if I get to *five*

if I get to *five*

WHAT CHILDREN CAN

TEACH US ABOUT

COURAGE AND CHARACTER

Fred Epstein, M.D.,

and Joshua Horwitz

A Living Planet Book

HENRY HOLT AND COMPANY · NEW YORK

In order to protect their privacy,
the names of some people have been changed.

Henry Holt and Company, LLC
Publishers since 1866
115 West 18th Street
New York, New York 10011

Henry Holt® is a registered trademark of
Henry Holt and Company, LLC.

Copyright © 2003 by Fred Epstein and Joshua Horwitz
All rights reserved.
Distributed in Canada by H. B. Fenn and Company Ltd.

Library of Congress Cataloging-in-Publication Data
Epstein, Fred, date.
    If I get to five : what children can teach us about courage and
character / Fred Epstein and Joshua Horwitz.—1st ed.
        p. cm.
    ISBN 0-8050-7144-X
    1. Epstein, Fred, date. 2. Neurosurgeons—United States—
Biography. 3. Pediatric surgeons—United States—Biography.
4. Tumors in children—Patients—United States. 5. Courage.
6. Character. I. Horwitz, Joshua. II. Title.

RD592.9.E67 A3 2003
617.4'8'092—dc21
[B]   2002038793

Henry Holt books are available for special promotions
and premiums. For details contact: Director, Special Markets.

First Edition 2003
Designed by Victoria Hartman
Printed in the United States of America
1   3   5   7   9   10   8   6   4   2

To Kathy

—F.E.

To my father,

Norman Horwitz, M.D.

—J.H.

Fall seven times, stand up eight.

—Japanese proverb

Contents

if I get to *five*

Prologue

The title of this book was inspired by a child who helped me through one of my first moments of truth as a pediatric neurosurgeon. Naomi was only four years old when she arrived at the hospital in grave condition. She had a complicated brain tumor that was wrapped around two arteries, one of which had already bled inside her cranium and sent her into a coma.

This was twenty-five years ago, when pediatric neurosurgery was in its infancy as a surgical specialty. We had relatively unsophisticated tools for imaging and extracting tumors, and not a lot of experience on which to draw. I had few surgical options for treating Naomi, none of them good. I knew I had to do something quickly or else she'd certainly die. I decided to operate in two stages; first I would relieve the pressure of the bleed and buy us both some time, and then, if she came out of her coma, I'd operate a second time to remove the tumor.

After the initial surgery, Naomi regained consciousness. Even with her head swathed in bandages, she was a feisty kid with dancing eyes and a willfulness I'd rarely seen in adults. During my first conversation with her, she climbed to her feet and announced defiantly: "If I get to five, I'm going to learn to ride a two-wheeler!"

I'd see Naomi each day on rounds as we waited for her to regain her strength for the second surgery. While I reviewed her chart, she'd stand up on her bed and update me on her plans. On Monday: "If I get to five, I'm going to beat my older brother at tic-tac-toe." On Tuesday: "If I get to five, I'm going to learn to tie my shoes with a double knot!"

I was always relieved that Naomi never asked me if I thought she'd get to five. In my own mind, her odds weren't good. She had the kind of tumor that made me wish for divine guidance—or at least for more self-confidence and skill than I possessed. As the second, more difficult operation approached, I grew increasingly anxious—and Naomi grew ever more determined in her daily proclamations: "If I get to five, I'm going to learn to read the comics." "If I get to five, I'm going to jump rope—backward!"

As I faced off against a frightening kind of tumor for the first time, I found myself drawing courage from this four-year-old girl. She intuited that even though she had revived from a coma, getting to five was still an "if," not a "when," proposition. She grasped that to get to five, she needed to look forward to the next level of mastery—learning to jump rope, learning to read.

Naomi taught me that the child's determination to embrace the next stage in life, to become more powerful and master new skills, can be a lifetime asset. She reminded me that whenever I ran up against a tumor that had "inoperable" stamped across it, I needed to focus on the child whose life was on the line. That was a crucial lesson for me at a formative stage of my career. It strengthened my resolve never to give up on a child, no matter how daunting the course appeared.

Children are geniuses at raising the bar for themselves, clearing it, and then setting it one notch higher. Working with children raises the bar for me, and for everyone else whose lives they touch. They inspire us to dig deeper for the strength to do what feels hardest, what's scariest. And to do that, we have to once again become young at heart.

Much has been written about how important it is for adults to model behavior for children. What I've discovered again and again is that *children can model courage and character for adults,* if only we pay attention to them.

People tend to think of children as weak and vulnerable, as fragile little people. In my experience, they're giants. They have immense and open hearts. Their minds can expand to encompass any reality. Their bodies and souls are amazingly resilient. And their spirits can soar in the face of enormous physical and psychic pain. What we often mistake for fragility in children is their openness to experience. I believe it's this quality of openness—of heart, mind, and spirit—that makes children so resilient in the face of life-threatening illnesses, or any other obstacle in their path.

I don't mean to romanticize childhood—it was the most difficult period of my own life—or to dismiss the many ways that children depend on adults for protection and guidance. But what we so easily forget is that a child's resilience is a birthright we all once shared. I believe that the wellspring of childhood strength lives on within us as adults, and that we can draw on this inner resource to confront adversity at any stage of life.

Throughout my career as a pediatric neurosurgeon, my young patients have been my most trustworthy teachers and guides. At critical junctures in my life, they've shown me the way toward compassion, hope, tenacity, and, most of all, courage. On countless occasions I've witnessed displays of uncommon courage by kids whose biggest anxieties should be a math exam.

We all wonder what we're made of; these kids have found out. They've been tested in ways most adults can't imagine. Along the way, they've learned the kind of hard-knocks lessons that we pray every day to be spared. I believe that their remarkable journeys will inspire anyone who is struggling to prevail over a crisis that tests their courage and faith.

My career has afforded me a rare and privileged window into what young people are capable of accomplishing when they confront their worst fears. Every day when I've gone to work, I've felt as if I was going to school. It's where children have taught me most of what I know about character, about the sacredness of every human life, and about the awesome, almost unstoppable power of the life force.

An important part of my ongoing education in the art of resilience has come via a steady stream of cards and letters from my patients, often with hand-inscribed photos attached, sometimes with a clipping from a local newspaper enclosed by a proud parent. While every child's story is unique in its particulars, the themes have been recurrent, whether the writer hailed from Norwalk, Connecticut; Hyden, Kentucky; or New Delhi, India. They all expressed shock, disbelief, and some level of self-pity when they were first diagnosed with a life-threatening illness. But in the course of surviving their crisis, or at least adjusting to an ongoing state of crisis, they gained life-changing insights.

The lessons encoded in these letters have little to do with disease and death. They are simple and profound truths about unexpected inner strengths revealed in times of crisis: the courage to endure in the face of pain, the redeeming value of life lived in the present, and the power of love and faith to transcend all boundaries, even death.

I've never subscribed to the belief that suffering is ennobling or illuminating. The "gift of misfortune" or the "gift of cancer" mind-set that characterizes so much survivor literature has always struck me as a rationalization. To my mind, disease and premature death are an insult to life, which is why I've committed my career to battling them. But in these letters, and in the conversations and e-mails that followed, I discovered one undeniable, irreducible blessing: buried inside the soil of grief and loss lay a seed of hope—and from this seed, new life could sprout and grow.

As I now realize, I have received much more from my young patients than I have given. Their openness—to new ideas, to love, and to faith—has opened my own mind, my own heart, and my own spirit. This book is written in tribute to the open path that children offer us, if we only dare to follow them.

NAOMI SURVIVED HER SECOND SURGERY. SHE GOT TO five, and never looked back. Though she suffered some brain damage from her tumor, Naomi never felt sorry for herself or ashamed of her deficits.

Today she's a happy, thirty-year-old woman who loves life. Her job as a grocery store clerk may not seem impressive compared to the careers of other young women, but Naomi is enormously proud of her accomplishments. She writes me silly, affectionate letters that begin, "Dear Freddy Boy," in which she proudly updates me on where she's working and what she's doing. When she's in Manhattan, she drops by to say hello and to make me laugh.

Naomi made the most out of an unhappy accident of birth—a tumor that grew slowly inside her brain for four years before announcing itself. I've thought about her a lot recently, as I've struggled to cope with a particularly nasty incident in my own life.

On a Sunday morning in late September 2001, I went out for my usual twenty-mile bike ride near my home in Connecticut. That afternoon I was planning to take two of my boys to a Giants football game. I never got there.

I've been told that the front tire of my bicycle hit a depression in the pavement, and I pitched forward over the handlebars. I landed on the pavement headfirst. The impact knocked my brain against the back of my skull, tearing a blood vessel, which caused bleeding over the surface of the brain. I was rushed to the nearest trauma center where a neurosurgeon who happened to be on call was able to remove the blood clot and relieve the pressure on my brain. Although I was wearing a helmet, what truly saved my life was the prompt and expert medical attention I received.

I remained in a coma for twenty-six days.

When I finally regained consciousness, I could only open one eye partway and wiggle my left big toe. I could see my wife, Kathy, and feel her hand holding mine, but I couldn't talk. I couldn't even breathe without the assistance of a ventilator.

I was totally helpless. What I knew was that I couldn't afford to become hopeless.

From years of treating serious head injuries, I was well versed in the rehabilitation drill, and it was no picnic. First I'd have to be weaned off the ventilator. Then I'd have to learn to swallow. And talk. And walk. I knew I'd have my wife by my side every step of the way, smiling encouragement and squeezing my hand. But I also understood it was going to be a long uphill climb. And no one besides Kathy was likely to believe I'd make it.

The policeman who came to our house an hour after I was taken to the hospital had told Kathy, "It's critical. Hurry." When I didn't come out of my coma that first week, I'm sure most people—including many of my colleagues who knew the odds—wrote me off for dead. Others thought I would be consigned to what's referred to as a "perpetual vegetative state." The survival rate for an injury like mine is only 20 percent, and only a few emerge from trauma-induced comas after twenty-six days. When they do, their prognosis is grim—especially when they're in their sixties, as I am. Young people tend to do better; their brains are more resilient. I like to think my brain is younger than its biological age because I've always been mentally and physically active. Or maybe I'm just bullheaded.

A week after I revived from my coma, I was moved to a rehabilitation hospital in Manhattan. Gradually—and until I went through rehab for a head injury myself, I never truly grasped the meaning of the word—I began to recover my basic brain functions. I learned to breathe on my own. I learned to swallow. I learned to talk—first in single, barely audible words, then in halting sentences. Right now, I'm learning to walk, one baby step at a time.

As I begin work on this book, I'm back at my own hospital, Beth Israel—not as a doctor but as a patient. After six months at the rehab hospital I was restless to get back to my home base. I still have months of intensive rehab ahead of me. Each day is a grind: speech therapy, followed by occupational therapy, followed by cognitive therapy, followed by physiotherapy for my weak arm and leg. My mind is clear and my spirit is willing, but parts of my body are still not patched into my brain correctly. My right arm and leg are still partially paralyzed, my speech is still slurred, and I have double vision. With time, and more hard work, they'll improve.

Meanwhile, I have to raise the bar another notch for myself every day. I find myself chanting my own "If I get to" mantras to coax myself through the next long session of rehab. If I rehab my right arm well enough, I can play catch with my sons in the backyard. If I get back on my feet, I can sail my boat again on Long Island Sound. If I get my voice back to full strength, I can argue cases with the other doctors at the weekly tumor conferences on the first floor. If I get back to my old self, I can be a surgeon again.

1

Hold Someone's Hand

We can do no great things;
only small things with great love.

—Mother Teresa

Twenty years after my encounter with Naomi, I was at the top of my field. I ran one of the world's premier pediatric neurosurgical services at New York University. I'd earned a national and international reputation by figuring out how to operate on tumors in children's brain stems and spinal cords—two areas that had previously been considered inoperable. My peers had elected me president of every major organization in my field. In sum, I had all the status and material perks that come with being a star surgeon in a medical star system.

I was headed for a fall. I just didn't see it coming.

All my life I'd been mesmerized by technology. I was never much of a student, but I always had an affinity for machines. As a boy I loved building elaborate model airplanes. When I grew up I remained enchanted by cars, planes, boats, and trains. I liked to unwind from the stresses of surgery by play-ing with remote-control cars or trains in my backyard. (One of my favorite grown-up toys is a scale-model electric train set that runs outdoors, even in the rain.)

When I trained in neurosurgery, I became intrigued by the technical obstacles to operating in the brain stem and spinal cord—and by the tools that might make it possible. The brain stem of an adult is only about the size of your thumb—in a child's brain it's even smaller. This tiny portion of the brain controls all our basic life functions: consciousness, breathing, balance, blood pressure, temperature control, eye movement, hearing, and swallowing. It's also the main crossroad for all the major nerve pathways running to and from the cognitive and sensory areas of the brain. For some reason that we don't understand, children develop more tumors in the brain stem than adults do. But because it's the seat of so many critical functions, there's precious little room for error during surgery. The same goes for operating on tumors inside the spinal cord, which is filled with fragile nerve pathways connecting the brain to the rest of the body. One wrong move and your patient is paralyzed.

Before the 1970s, we simply didn't have the tools or the techniques to operate in these areas with any margin of safety. But like so much of medicine in the past few decades, neuro-surgery has been revolutionized by technological advances. New imaging techniques like CT (computerized tomography) scans and MRI (magnetic resonance imaging) transformed our ability to identify and locate tumors. The operating microscope magnified viscous white and gray matter into identifiable tumor structures. The stainless-steel scalpel gave way to high-vibration wands that could liquefy and suction out tiny tumors; then came focused radiation scalpels like the Gamma Knife that could perform even finer work in sensitive areas.

All these advances created opportunities for attacking tumors in locations where surgeons had never dared to venture. For someone like me, who felt most in command when I had a machine in my grasp, this was a terrifically exciting time to be a neurosurgeon. During the 1980s I came up with new uses for existing surgical technologies and created innovative procedures for resecting tumors that no one else wanted to touch. I virtually lived at the hospital, operating on hundreds of brain and spinal cord tumors a year. I couldn't get enough of it. I became the consummate technologist, thoroughly enamored of the beauty and power of medicine's high-tech tools. And why not? They enabled my team to increase our cure rate from 20 percent to over 50 percent in just twenty years. Solving some of the technical problems of pediatric neurosurgery gave me everything I'd ever wanted from work: intellectual challenge, the recognition of my peers, financial security, and, most of all, the chance to save young lives.

My success made me arrogant enough to perceive technology as an end in itself.

My wake-up call came in the form of a letter from the grave, written by a seventeen-year-old boy who had been my patient. Chris Lambert was a wonderfully talented and bright teenager—he had charisma and smarts and a big heart. And he had a malignant brain tumor that wouldn't quit. I took it out; it grew back. I took it out again; it grew back again. Chris had the kind of tumor I came to hate—a rapacious, malignant growth that was sucking the life out of him. In the end, I ran out of medical options, and Chris ran out of time.

A short time after he died, Chris's mother mailed me a copy of a poem he had written two weeks before his death. As I read it, I could hear Chris's voice in my head:

I have for many useless hours contemplated eternity.
I have prayed in the night
By the cold and lonely side of my bed
For the peace and strength of our living God.
And I still wonder: Will I be saved?
I wait with hope in my heart.

I am struggling, O Lord, to stay alive
I am losing my sacred strength
I am living a life of confusion
And death is very near.
I ask you reader, whoever you may be,
Take my trembling hand and warm it with care and sympathy.

I believe that love is the sole purpose of man's life
And without love life is sterile and without meaning.

But with love life has wonder.
With love life has color and beauty.

Reading that poem demolished me. It still does when I read it today. I had failed him. I had done everything I could to save his life, but I had ignored his deepest emotional need—to feel loved. His words haunted me: "I ask you reader, whoever you may be, take my trembling hand and warm it with care and sympathy." I hadn't heard his plea until it was too late. How many other children had I turned a deaf ear to in their hour of need?

I realized that by working single-mindedly for decades to become the consummate medical technologist, I had traveled down a blind alley. I had lost sight of what was most human in my patients—their need for comfort. Why hadn't I seen that even the best technology can't soothe a child's fear and loneliness?

It had been so easy for me to fall in love with medical technology. It seemed to solve so many problems. Why had it been so much harder for me to give that love to a dying child?

I went into a tailspin. Losing a patient was always devastating, but it came with the job description, and I'd learned to buck up and go back into the OR. This time was different. I hadn't just lost a patient—I had lost my balance. I had spent my whole career putting technology on a pedestal—a pedestal I'd gladly shared—and now it had been kicked out from under me.

I had to figure out how to get back on my feet and start over.

I had always championed an open-minded approach to surgical problems. I was the let's-try-anything-that-might-work guy. Now, at an advanced stage in my medical career, Chris turned me around to the possibility of a more open-*hearted* path.

I began to contemplate a different kind of healing environment—a pediatric unit where emotional intelligence mattered as much as technical expertise, where sick kids wouldn't have to stop being children just because they were in a hospital, where any child or parent could reach out for someone's hand to hold.

This idea took root in my imagination. Why not create a state-of-the-art medical facility that was both kid-friendly and family-friendly? It could be a sanctuary that offered families all the medical and personal support that they needed for healing. Not just from the medical staff but from psychologists, social workers, chaplains, music therapists, child development specialists—even a clown!

It was just a daydream, until the afternoon I got a phone call from the chairman of the Board of Trustees of Beth Israel Medical Center. He offered me the chance to build a neuroscience service from the ground up. No limits. No boundaries. If I had a blank check, he asked, what would I create?

I told him about my dream of building a top-flight medical facility where patients, their families, their doctors, and their nurses could work together as a team, where cutting-edge care didn't start and end in the operating room, where no families would be turned away because their case was too hopeless or their finances too limited.

"Okay," he said. "Let's do it."

I leapt at the offer. At the time, I was the chief of pediatric neurosurgery at New York University Medical Center, a prestigious and high-profile unit. Plenty of people told me I was crazy to walk away from all the institutional security NYU represented. Strangely, I never felt more secure than the day I decided to leave and begin building something from scratch.

I embarked on this adventure at a stage of my career when most surgeons are planning for their retirement. But I felt younger and more energized than I had in years. Chris's poem reminded me of why I became a doctor in the first place. My parents were both committed do-gooders: my mom was a social worker with seriously socialist leanings; my dad was part of that first, idealistic generation of psychoanalysts who believed they could cure the world of mental illness. I had wanted to heal the world with the same sense of purpose as my parents. Somewhere along the way, I'd drifted off course.

Now I'd been given a chance most people don't get—to do it over and get it right, if not for Chris, then for all the other sick and frightened children who would cross my path.

Over the next few months, I discovered that there was a lot more thwarted idealism among my peers than I ever imagined.

When I made the move to Beth Israel, 108 highly trained and accomplished doctors, nurses, and medical professionals left with me to launch the Institute for Neurology and Neurosurgery (the INN). Like me, they had all gone into medicine with idealistic goals, only to find that so much of medicine today—even at the best medical centers—is practiced in a hierarchical atmosphere where doctors stand aloof from nurses and other health care professionals, where surgeons compete with each other more than they collaborate, where patients are treated as "cases" rather than as human beings in crisis. Over time, your idealism drains away and cynicism starts to seep in to fill the void.

What excited us was the opportunity to take our careers down a more compassionate path. Surgeons, and even nurses, have a tendency to compartmentalize their professional and emotional lives. We're trained to believe that we can best serve our patients by remaining objective professionals. With so much fear and anxiety swirling around our patients and their families, it's easy to imagine that responding to all their emotional needs would be overwhelming, and might even erode one's professional judgment.

Now, six years down the open-hearted road, my colleagues and I have reached a paradoxical conclusion: we've become *better* healers—more compassionate, more resilient, and more creative problem-solvers. The closer we've gotten to our patients and their families, the more strength and inspiration we've been able to draw from them. And by keeping our hearts, as well as our minds, open to our young patients, we've learned professional and personal lessons that eluded us earlier in our careers.

We've learned that keeping ourselves open to the emotional as well as physical pain around us doesn't come naturally; retreating from other people's pain does. Compassion isn't a passive state. It's an act of will, an act of courage: the courage to cope with every parent's worst nightmare, the courage to be emotionally honest, the courage to risk having your heart broken, the courage to care enough to push yourself to do what's scariest.

I used to think that courage meant taking on the toughest cases, being the guy who dared to make the life-and-death judgment calls in the operating room. I now know that holding a child's hand while he undergoes chemotherapy can be a lot scarier than holding his life in my hands during an operation.

I don't want to give the impression that I turned my back on technology. The three operating theaters at the INN are the best equipped in the world. We have all the coolest tools, and our surgeons are technical wizards. But you can buy technology out of a catalogue, and I can train any reasonably intelligent doctor to become a good technical surgeon. Compassion you can't buy, or teach. If you're raised right, you learn it from your parents when you're young. If you're lucky, you get a refresher course from a kid like Chris.

THERE'S A CLASSIC CHILDREN'S STORY ABOUT MAKING something from nothing, called "Stone Soup." Three soldiers come to an impoverished village and, using the power of suggestion and imagination, they persuade the stingy villagers to help them build a glorious soup from a simple "stock" the soldiers have concocted out of water and stone. By the end of the story, each villager has managed to find some vegetables or grains or meat to throw into the pot. The delicious moral of this tale is that even in times of scarcity a rich feast is possible—so long as we each bring something to the table.

In a pediatric neurosurgical ward, there's no escaping the raw reality of sick children. The stakes couldn't be higher, and there are never enough answers to the tough questions we face. Sometimes it feels like we're trying to make soup from water and stones. But somehow, we always seem to get a hot meal on the table. Parents, doctors, nurses, therapists—and most of all, the children—dig deep inside and find something nourishing or comforting to contribute.

One of the secret ingredients in our stone soup has been our music therapist, Tina Breschia. During the INN's first five years, Tina entered the emotional vortex of a child's sickroom armed only with a guitar and her determination to make the pain go away. Tina also brought the healing power of music into the children's play center, the weekly prayer sessions, and our annual memorial service. Most of the medicines we use work better for some patients than for others. Music seems to be a universal balm that crosses every boundary of culture and age. Children aren't the only ones who respond to music. Parents crave its comfort and release as well.

Here's how Tina explains the magical science of music therapy: "On a level of physics, music actually moves the air in the room; our bodies receive and perceive music's movement. We need our emotions to move through us and music can be a catalyst for allowing that movement. Sometimes silence can be so painful, so still. Music helps circulate the emotions in a room—and in a person's heart."

I've seen firsthand how Tina's music can clear the stifled emotional air of a child's sickroom. Carmen and Julietta were both four-year-old daughters of recent immigrants; Carmen's parents were from Mexico, Julietta's were from El Salvador. These two girls both loved to sing and dance, and soon became friends. They both had brain tumors.

While they were going through chemotherapy together, Tina used to come and play music for the girls and their families. Tina spoke almost no Spanish and the girls spoke no English, but Tina used her music to build bridges to these girls, and between their two families. She sang a Spanish folk song called "Somos El Barco" ("We Are the Boat"). The chords she played on her guitar from Pachelbel's Canon in D offered a soothing counterpoint to the grim monotone of the IV drips.

The girls were both on the same postoperative chemo

protocol. It worked for Carmen; her tumor shrank and she recovered. Julietta's tumor grew back, crowding the life from her small body. As Julietta became frail and approached death, Carmen and her mother came back to the hospital every day to visit.

During one of Julietta's last days, her family asked Tina to visit her room. This was not an uncommon request. As a child's death draws near, everyone's heart fills with despair. What's left to do when medicine and prayers fail? Sometimes the most comforting thing we can do is to hold hands, sing songs, and play music.

When Tina arrived, Julietta was cradled in her mother's lap. Her father stood motionless at the window, facing outside and crying quietly. Tina sat down across from Julietta and her mother and played a quiet song on her guitar, "La Mar Estaba Serena" ("The Sea Was Calm").

Carmen and her mother arrived and went right over to Julietta. Carmen's mother cried and hugged Julietta's mother from behind. She kissed Julietta on the forehead. Carmen stood beside Julietta and caressed her arm and gazed into her eyes. In her young life Carmen had witnessed a lot of pain; she'd already lost another friend on the ward. Along the way, she'd learned a lot about comfort and care.

Carmen looked around and saw that all of the grown-ups in the room were crying. So she began to play. She sat on the floor and started to stir a pot of hot soup in her lap. After adding salt and pepper, she held the soup bowl up to Julietta's mother. Carmen dipped her pretend spoon into the soup, blew on it to cool it off, and held it up to the tearful woman, whispering, *"Para ti"* ("For you").

The mother smiled and took a sip. Rising carefully to her feet, so as not to spill, Carmen carried her bowl over to where Julietta's father stood by the window. She tugged on his shirt, then lifted the spoon toward his mouth. Emerging for a moment out of the depth of his misery, he crouched down beside Carmen.

"Es bueno para ti" ("It's good for you"), said Carmen.

He tasted the soup and nodded back in agreement, *"Si, esta bueno."*

WHEN WE SAT DOWN TO DESIGN THE INN, WE TRIED TO rethink the traditional medical culture and reinvent the healing environment. Beyond providing the best surgical services, our goal was to reach out to children and their families in small, low-tech ways that would make their experience less clinical and more humane.

We wanted to make the INN as family friendly as possible, so we invited parents to advise us on how best to furnish and decorate the rooms. They recommended daybeds and washing machines, so they could sleep in with their kids and wash their own clothes without having to leave the hospital. We decided there would be no set visiting hours on our unit. Family and friends could come and go whenever they wanted, and parents could sleep over with children in their rooms. Dogs and other pets were welcome too.

We decided to hire staff musicians and entertainers to keep things lively. We tried to relieve some of the stress by offering yoga and massage—to the staff as well as the families. We offered pastoral care and held interdenominational religious services where children, parents, physicians, nurses, and staff members could pray together.

We also wanted to smooth the rough edges off the grim business of pediatric neurosurgery. Since all kids are hypersensitive about how their hair looks, we would always shave the smallest possible area of their scalp before we operated. We let young children drive themselves to the operating room in electric cars. Parents could accompany their children into the OR and hold them until they were asleep. Kids were encouraged to bring their stuffed animals with them into surgery. (When one kid halted at the door of the OR and insisted, "I'm not going in without the clown!" we paged our resident clown, Adam Auslander, and told him he was needed in the OR, on the double.) Instead of waking up alone in the recovery room, facing a wall of beeping monitors, we made sure that a child's parents were the first thing she saw when she regained consciousness. We disguised IV poles as palm trees.

Most important of all, we committed to making ourselves

available to patients and their families. To this end, I wanted to make the environment as informal and accessible as possible. Our doors stay open whenever we're not seeing patients. Patients and their families often deal with us on a first-name basis. (My own office door has "Fred" written across it in big letters.) We don't talk over their heads in medical jargon. We don't wear white coats. I give out my home number to patients and their families because I know how important a doctor's accessibility is to peace of mind. Giving my patients this power goes a long way toward soothing their anxiety, and I find it's a power they rarely abuse. When they call me at home, it's because they need to, because they're scared out of their wits or in pain. In which case, I want to hear from them.

I can't prove that a humane approach to patient care has improved their medical outcomes in terms of longevity. But I know that having their medical team unconditionally on their side has made my patients and their families better able to survive and recover emotionally. I've learned that we can't measure results simply in quantitative terms of morbidity and mortality. Disease is a *qualitative* crisis that requires a fully human response. When a child develops a brain tumor, it's like a bomb going off in a family. Shock waves ripple out in every direction, leveling any semblance of normalcy. For these families to heal, they need the support of a committed team of care providers.

Like any extended family, we share a lot of tears and sorrow; we also share a lot of laughter and joy. Often it gets rowdy—patients and their doctors like to play ball games with each other in the hallways—and at times it's downright undignified. One of our clown's most requested routines is called the Butt Dance, what Adam refers to proudly as "a cheap bit well done." He basically shakes his booty to music from a boom box that's attached to his waist. It gets a lot of laughs, and kids love to join in.

One day Adam was goofing around with a very sick nine-year-old boy. Ricky wanted to do the Butt Dance in the hallway with Adam and see how many people they could get to join them. "Let's see if we can set the World Indoor Record for the Butt Dance," Ricky hollered, grabbing his IV tree and pushing it into the hallway. So they started down the hall, boom box and kazoos blaring, shaking their butts with abandon. They quickly picked up a couple of kids as they passed the adjoining rooms. Then they collared a few patients and siblings in the waiting room, then a nurse at the nursing station. When they proceeded past the doctors' offices, they got an oncologist on board. I won't say who; he's got a fancy reputation to preserve. By the time they got to the reception desk they had eighteen people doing the Butt Dance in parade. I don't know if that's the World Indoor Record, but it's definitely the Beth Israel Record.

THERE'S A STRONG LINK BETWEEN PLAY AND COMFORT. At the INN, it's a bridge that children and adults are constantly leading each other across. Honey Shields is our director of Child Life on the tenth floor. She's also every patient's extra mom, and the most compassionate person I know. She truly loves without boundaries. When a visitor to the playroom asks Honey if she has any children of her own, she replies, "These *are* my children." And they are.

Honey runs the play programs for the kids, making sure they can celebrate all the holidays inside the unit, helping them shoot videotape movies, keeping the playroom a place of joy and laughter. But it's hard to describe everything she does, because she seems to take care of everyone—the children, their parents, the stressed-out staff. Honey will gently remind a mother in the playroom who's close to tears that it's important to cry, but not in front of her child, because a child can't handle watching her mother go to pieces. Then she'll invite her to the parents' lounge where they cry together, and then hold ice chips against their eyes before returning to the playroom.

Last year, Honey got a phone call from a mother of one of our success stories. Tara came in three years ago with a life-threatening brain stem tumor. Now she's cured, living at home on Long Island and going to school like any eight-year-old. But Tara still has some residual facial paralysis that makes her very self-conscious around her classmates.

Tara's mother explained to Honey that it's been hard for Tara to make close friends. What upset Tara most was that she didn't have anyone to invite home for a sleepover. So that afternoon Honey went out and bought a pair of pink pajamas for Tara and a matching pair for herself. Then she took the train to Long Island and had a sleepover with Tara. They played with Barbies, slept in a tent in the living room, and had chocolate pancakes for breakfast. Later that morning Honey changed from her pink pajamas into her grown-up clothes and came back to work.

Every day at the INN we enter the unknown, where terrible or wonderful things can happen, where unanswerable questions such as "Why do innocent children get sick?" lurk behind every patient's door. Getting your feelings hurt is an occupational hazard of loving children, but kids are also expert at mending hearts.

David Rawlings was a sophomore at Columbia University who loved to play basketball, despite his chronic back pain. When it eventually became too painful for him to sit through classes, he came to the hospital for some tests. The scans revealed a tumor near the top of his spine, which I was able to operate on and remove.

In the days just before and after surgery, David kept up a hearty front. Every evening a different group of friends crowded into his room for a party. It was like a frat house in there. Then his post-op therapy started to take its toll. The steroids we prescribed to control the swelling in the spinal cord made his face puff up. We were radiating the remnants of his high spinal tumor, which made his hair start to fall out. Medically, he had a good prognosis, but his vanity was gravely injured. He told his friends to stop coming around. The only people he'd let in to visit were his parents and his sister. As his treatment continued, he became withdrawn and depressed.

Then one day, a seven-year-old girl named Louise wandered into David's room. She had pale blue eyes and hair the color of a bright copper penny. She stood just inside the doorway, staring at David until he looked up from his *Sports Illustrated.* Louise asked him why he never left his room, not even to play video games in the children's lounge. Why didn't he come eat cake and ice cream at the birthday parties? David was embarrassed to have a kid asking him the question all the adults had been dancing around for a week. "I'm going bald," he shrugged. "I look like a clown."

Louise bent her head down to reveal a scar at its base. "I had a tumor, right here," she said, pointing to her scar. "The doctor took it away, but they're still giving me medicine." Then she ran her hand through her hair and gave it a gentle tug. A clump of hair came out in her hand. "See?" she said, matter-of-factly. "It's just hair. What's the big deal?"

That was the last day David spent feeling sorry for himself. "I figured if this little girl could handle losing her hair, why should I get freaked out about it? I had tougher fights ahead of me. Louise got it right: it *was* just hair, and eventually it grew back. Lucky for me, my tumor didn't."

YOU CAN'T SPEND YOUR CAREER WORKING WITH SICK children without wondering, "How can this be? Who the hell's in charge here?" Something as unforgivable and incomprehensible as tumors growing in children's bodies makes you inquire into areas beyond rational explanation.

Some people look to religious parables to help understand why the world is so full of pain. The Book of Job. The serpent in the Garden. Personally, I've always found more wisdom and solace in fairy tales. Ever since I was a child they've spoken to me about the dark and scary side of nature, and human nature. They affirm that evil *does* exist—but that it's not indomitable. No matter how frightening the stories, they always preserve the promise of good winning out over evil. I liked the fact that no witch or ogre was ever so powerful that a child's pluck and courage couldn't ensure a happy ending. It's probably why I named my boat—which has always been my safe haven from the jagged edges of hospital life—the *Ever After.*

When my kids were younger, reading fairy tales was our favorite bedtime ritual. One I liked most helped explain how evil comes into the world, how it threatens to freeze our hearts, and how it can be vanquished by the love of a young girl: Hans Christian Andersen's *The Snow Queen.* It tells the story of a wicked hobgoblin who creates a warped looking glass that reflects everything beautiful in the world as ugly, distorts everything good into evil. One day, the mirror falls to

the ground and breaks into a million pieces. The tiny frag-
ments of glass float through the air. One silver splinter lodges
in the eye of a young boy named Kay and freezes his heart
into a lump of ice. Kay turns against his lifelong playmate and
devoted friend, Gerda, mocking her mercilessly and tearing a
rose from her garden. The first blizzard of winter arrives, bringing with it the Snow Queen. The Snow Queen lashes Kay's
little sled to hers and whisks him off to her distant ice palace.

Early the next spring, little Gerda journeys far and wide
across the frozen tundra until she finds Kay imprisoned in the
Snow Queen's palace. At first he stares at her coldly, without
love or recognition. But Gerda's warm teardrops melt his
frozen heart. Kay begins to cry himself and the glass splinter
falls from his eye. Kay and Gerda gallop home on the back of
a reindeer, their everlasting friendship redeemed and renewed.

For the children I treat, and their families, the diagnosis of
a brain tumor shatters their lives into countless tiny pieces.
Happiness and wholeness seem irretrievably lost. As one
mother described that fateful moment to me, "I stepped over
the threshold, forever banished from the Mothers-of-Healthy-
Children Club. I'd sit there listening to them complain—
about how they were up half the night with their child's cold,
about how their kid can't read well and has to get tutoring—
wishing I could still be in that club, and feeling angry that I
can't."

As often as not, it's the children who lead the family out of despair. Though it's the parents' job to show strength, it's usually the children who start picking up the pieces and rebuilding their lives. I can't tell you how many parents report, with a mixture of pride and shame, how they found themselves drawing courage and hope from their six-year-old daughter or twelve-year-old son.

Then something extraordinary happens. These young people, who have experienced the fragility of life firsthand, become acutely sensitized to the suffering of *other* people in crisis, the fragility of *other* people's lives. They instinctively reach out and do whatever they can to repair the damage they see around them, one broken fragment at a time. Some of them do it in simple ways, such as comforting another child or another parent. Many of them, after recovering their own health, return to hospital settings to volunteer to work with sick kids. Others take a leadership role in organizing groups and launching initiatives to help kids in need. Whatever the scale of their work, they set about the serious, heartfelt job of healing the world, one life at a time. They redeem the suffering in their own lives, and inspire other people to do the same.

Mischa Zimmerman's life broke apart seven years ago. At thirteen, he was a beautiful boy, a great athlete and student, a popular kid with nothing but clear sky above him.

Then came the symptoms—in his case vomiting and weight loss—and eventually the diagnosis: a tumor that had penetrated his brain stem. His mother, Heni, had been diagnosed with cancer six months earlier, and Mischa's illness sent his family into a deepening crisis. "My own mother was a Holocaust survivor," Heni recounts, "so I grew up with stories of the camps. The hopelessness and the terror. When this happened to Mischa, I understood how it must have been in the camps. It felt like someone had a gun to my head day and night."

Mischa had his first surgery in a hospital in New Jersey. For almost six months following surgery he remained imprisoned in what's called a "locked-in" state. He was awake and aware of the world around him, but he was totally paralyzed and incapable of communicating. At first he couldn't move a muscle. Then, he could move one foot and signal yes or no with it in response to questions. A few months later, he could use his hands and spell out words on a letter-board. It was almost a year before he could begin to speak or to swallow food.

During his long "locked-in" months, Mischa believed that he was dead and that the limbo state he existed in was some kind of eerie afterworld. He could still see the world of the living going on around him, but he couldn't touch it or speak to it. "I remember seeing snow out the window and thinking, it must be winter in the living world," he recounts now. "It wasn't until months later, when I started to come out of it, that I realized I was still alive."

While Mischa was still recuperating a five-year-old boy down the hall asked Mischa if he could borrow *Toy Story*.

Mischa gave the tape to the boy as a gift. He still marvels at how this tiny event turned the boy around. "I couldn't believe how much something as small as a videotape meant to this kid. He hadn't smiled in a week, and here he was grinning and laughing out loud. I also realized how good it made me feel to do something for another kid. It made me feel more alive and less involved in my own problems. That's when I first had the idea for Kids Helping Kids."

While Mischa continued to fight to regain his health, he teamed up with his mother to launch Kids Helping Kids, a volunteer organization run by teens to benefit children and teens who are facing medical crises. The name of the group says it all—kids helping kids in whatever way they can: raising money to buy motorized wheelchairs, donating time to keep a lonely kid company in the hospital, pooling resources to grant a sick child a special wish.

Mischa began Kids Helping Kids by recruiting forty of his classmates at Montclair High School. He envisions growing this grass-roots program into a national network of young volunteers. "It's all about kids reaching out to each other," is how Mischa describes the group's mission. "I know from personal experience that no one can erase a kid's loneliness and sadness like another kid."

Mischa never set out to make his mark as an advocate or an activist. "Like everyone else, I just wanted to have a normal life, to be like other kids and fit in rather than stand out. But when you're in a wheelchair with a patch over one eye and your voice is messed up, it's impossible to blend in. So you get over it. You get over your inhibitions and your fears. There's not much that scares me now."

About the only thing that does scares Mischa, "a lot more than dying," he says, is the prospect of losing his independence. He attends New York University. He lives in a dormitory, takes care of himself, and navigates the streets of Greenwich Village in a motorized scooter. "When I'm asleep, I often dream that I'm not in a wheelchair. I'm normal, my old self. Then I wake up, and I have to come to grips with what's really going on in my life. I have to make today count."

Mischa keeps his emotional center of gravity by remembering the kids who need help more than he does. "When I was in the hospital and still locked in, there was a point where I wanted to blow my brains out. I figured that if I killed myself, I would get to move on from this limbo state to another world. Now suicide isn't in the picture. Even though a lot of things in my life suck, I can do things that other kids can't. A lot of people are worse off than me—and I can work to make their lives better."

During the months when he was still partially locked in, Mischa used to watch videos—the same dozen movies over and over again.

"The movie that really got me through that period was *The Shawshank Redemption*," he remembers. "I literally

35

watched that movie fifty or sixty times. Tim Robbins plays this guy whose wife is murdered. He's wrongfully accused of killing her and is thrown into one of those hellish maximum-security prisons. He has his whole life taken away from him; he has to subsist on hope—that's all he has. After twenty years in prison he finally escapes to freedom. I've always identified with that character. Like him, I keep hanging in there, trying to make a happy ending for my life, and for other people's lives."

I've played only a small part in Mischa's medical treatment, but he's taught me volumes about the potential for making one's personal redemption a blessing to others. Children have an instinct for redemption. They can find it in the most unlikely places. Even when their suffering is beyond our imagination, they can find a lifeline—even if they're locked inside a body with no companionship other than a stack of old videos.

Mischa understands that it's not what you *feel* that counts, it's what you *do* about it. He doesn't buy into the culture of T-shirt slogans and bumper-sticker ideologies that frame the world as a cosmic joke. *"Shit happens."* True enough, but it's how you behave in a shit-storm that shows what you're made of. *"Commit Random Acts of Kindness."* There's nothing random about acts of kindness. Compassion is an active verb with moral consequences.

When Mischa Zimmerman pulls himself out of his wheelchair to exhort a room full of high school students to open their hearts and donate their time and energy to helping other kids, he raises up everyone in the room. When he wheels into a hospital to give a bedridden little girl a new tricycle and a few words of encouragement, it's not a random act of kindness. It's a courageous and willful act of compassion that multiplies the good in the world—and helps heal a shattered life.

2

Live in the Moment

*The best thing about the future
is that is comes one day at a time.*

—Abraham Lincoln

I sometimes think of the INN as a through-the-looking-glass universe, where children are wise and brave beyond their years, where adults exist in an altered state of heightened emotion and attention. One of the most extreme distortions inside this particular looking glass is our sense of time.

On the one hand, it's just as hectic and harried here as the rest of the overscheduled world. There are never enough hours in the day. Patients are constantly arriving from around the country and across the globe, and they all need attention. Our waiting room is always crowded, we're always behind schedule, and our three ORs are often overbooked.

On a parallel but separate level, time slows to a virtual standstill. When a child is in pain, the minutes crawl by for her and her parents. When a family gets a bad diagnosis, the clock stops. On the great days, an operation can cure a kid and restart the clock. On a good day, it can buy some time for a sick child and his family. That's when each hour becomes as precious as the air we breathe. All that counts is life-in-the-moment.

The mother of a young patient of mine wrote me about how sweetly her family savored their time snatched back from the abyss:

> Eric's life has been difficult at times, but he has life! And for that we are eternally grateful. I take nothing for granted now. For me, there is nothing more wonderful than a perfectly ordinary day. The simple things in life feel especially exquisite; seeing Eric run and laugh, watching him climb into a school bus, seeing a popsicle melt down his chin, hearing his delight as he tears open a Christmas present. Because we never thought we would be allowed to witness these everyday miracles, they fill us with profound joy. And in this joy comes a more direct relationship with God, because in my heart I thank Him each time I can kiss, hold, feel and breathe my son.

No matter how many lives I may save, it's the children I can't rescue who haunt me. It's devastating to fight for a child's life and lose. I always feel responsible, as if I failed them and should have done more.

I've had to learn to accept that sometimes the most I can

give a child is the gift of time: one more summer at camp or one more year with her family. Though it never feels to me like enough, sometimes it is. This is a tough lesson for me, and for doctors like me, who were trained in a medical model that posited a cure as the only acceptable goal, and death as a failure.

I know better now. Calculating the value of a life in days and years is a fool's arithmetic; the only true measure of our lives is how richly we spend our allotted time, and how much of ourselves we share along the way.

Laura had just turned fifteen when an MRI revealed that her malignant tumor had grown back again for the third time. I was in a quandary about how to proceed. Operating again would buy her some time—but it wouldn't cure her condition, and she'd already been through two arduous operations and chemo protocols.

Like so many of my young patients, Laura had done a lot of accelerated growing up since her first operation at the age of twelve. While other teenagers were memorizing rock 'n' roll lyrics, Laura had become expert in chemotherapy and radiation protocols. Her parents were present whenever we had a formal consultation, but Laura always spoke for herself and took the lead in making treatment decisions.

I decided to tell her where we stood and to find out what she wanted to do. I'd long ago discovered that honesty isn't just the best policy with children—it's the only one that's possible if you want to maintain any trust in your relationship with them. The saddest, cruelest situations I've witnessed have been when children desperately want to know the truth about their condition, but their parents feel the need to protect them from it. Children invariably feel betrayed and angry.

I told Laura that I thought we could buy her some time with another operation.

She was equally straightforward in her response. "I'll tell you, Fred, I'm sick and tired of waking up in the recovery room with my head wrapped in a turban. I've had it with chemo and watching my hair fall out in my hands."

She looked up at her MRI films on the light box and sighed. "I'll tell you what I want. I really want to go back to horse-riding camp this summer. If I let you operate again, will I get the summer?"

I told her I felt confident she would.

"Okay, then," she said, flicking off the switch on the light box. "That's what I want you to do. But no more chemo."

That was in May. Laura recovered quickly from surgery and went off to camp in June. In July, I got a letter from her telling me all about the palomino she was riding and grooming that summer. In August, she wrote again—this time to describe with great pride a ribbon she won for show-jumping. She enclosed a snapshot of herself with her arms wrapped around the neck of a gleaming golden horse.

In September, when Laura came in for her checkup, she took me aside, away from her parents. She thanked me for keeping up my end of the deal and giving her the summer—the sunset trail rides, the morning walks alone with her horse.

Then Laura told me that her headaches were back. She died in October.

IT'S COMMON WISDOM THAT LIVING IN THE MOMENT IS the best way to master time. But it's hard for adults to seize the day the way children seem to do instinctively. We tend to fall into two opposing time traps.

The first is anxiety. We fear the passage of time and the loss it represents—aging, infirmity, death. Our fear of the future keeps us from pursuing our most cherished goals, while it erodes our ability to enjoy the present.

The second trap is complacency. Intellectually, we understand that our life is finite and could end suddenly at any time. But our fear of death is so powerful that we deny its inevitability. We lull ourselves into believing that there will always be a "later" when we can get around to whatever it is we've promised ourselves we'll do.

Sick children often acknowledge their mortality before their parents, or even their doctors, do. Like Laura, they often adopt a pragmatic attitude toward harvesting as much of life as their limited time allows. An eight-year-old boy who died on my unit last spring realized by midwinter that his time was very limited. Bobby made a list of what he most wanted to do before he died—ride in a convertible, ride in a fire engine, ride in a cement mixer—and he spent the spring methodically and joyfully working his way through his list. The day before he went into hospice, he checked off the last item on his wish list: riding in a float in a New York City parade.

When you're working around very sick kids, it's easy to become preoccupied with their disease and to lose sight of how fiercely alive they are, moment to moment. In-the-moment is where the play, the laughter, and the smiles are. The joy. Kids remind us in a hurry that all that's important, all that's real, is in the here and now. They have a way of showing us that there's something to celebrate in life at any moment.

A few years ago we had a six-year-old Greek patient named Eleni who had traveled from Athens for brain stem surgery. She had a good prognosis, but when I visited her on rounds a few days after surgery she still looked like a battle casualty—her head shaved and bandaged, her face puffed up with steroids. Her whole family appeared to be crammed into the room that afternoon, mostly wrinkled old women in long black dresses who didn't speak a word of English. It was like a wake in there. Everyone seemed to be in mourning. I explained through a young American relative that Eleni was doing fine, but her grandmother kept motioning tearfully to a "before" photo of Eleni on the night table, then pointing back at the little girl with sunken eyes and bandaged head.

When I spotted Adam, our staff clown, gallumphing down the hallway in oversized shoes, I dragged him into Eleni's room. It's not the kind of audience any performer is happy to take on, but Adam handled it like a pro. After quickly sizing up the scene, he pulled a handheld microphone from his over-sized belt and began to serenade Eleni with nonsense songs and ditties. He was singing gibberish, actually, but Eleni loved it. She clapped her hands and shouted for more. The old women in their long black dresses, however, didn't seem amused. They stared with bewilderment and anxiety at this strangely dressed clown, all the time fussing with the worry beads in their laps.

Then Adam offered the microphone to Eleni and invited her to join in the silliness. She gleefully took the mike and climbed out of bed. Some of the old women gasped with alarm, but when Eleni stepped onto the linoleum floor and started to sing, she was like Liza Minnelli playing the Copacabana. As she belted out a soulful Greek ballad, she had all of us spellbound. Then, with a masterful change of pace, she segued into an up-tempo song that had everyone tapping their feet and clapping their hands. Then she finished with what sounded like a Greek stand-up comedy routine. I have no idea what she said, but she managed to reduce a room full of old women to girlish laughter.

KIDS HAVE A SPECIAL GIFT—WE ALL HAD IT ONCE—THAT allows them to live in the moment while retaining a motivating vision of their future. I think of it as a form of stereoscopic vision that lets them simultaneously focus on the foreground and on the far horizon. They get an image in their heads about where they want to go, and then they put their heads down and concentrate on the next step in front of them.

The here and now is where life is richest and most immediate. But without a sense of purpose and destination we are doomed to paddle around in small, repetitive circles, or plunge over waterfalls we never saw coming.

I learned a lot about the guiding power of a personal vision from a young patient of mine who was born and raised in one of the worst housing projects in the Bronx. Karin grew up surrounded by poverty, crime, and decay in a single-parent household, sustained by a strong faith in God. At the age of ten she contracted bacterial spinal meningitis that reduced her weight to forty pounds and threatened her with permanent brain damage. Despite her doctors' predictions, she survived and recovered. It took her almost a year to walk, talk, and use her limbs again.

As a teenager, residual spinal fluid from her bout with meningitis led to hydrocephalus, a condition of excess spinal fluid inside the cranium that causes pressure on the brain. Once again she had to endure a painstaking recuperation. She learned to walk again. She kept on studying, even when she couldn't go to school. Many of her teachers didn't think she'd be able to graduate, but they were wrong. She went on to college, received an undergraduate degree with honors, a master's in communication arts, and is now three classes away from completing a master's degree in special education. Along the way, she also worked as an elementary school teacher.

Here's what Karin wrote to me about how her dream of a better future helped her see beyond a bleak present:

> I have always possessed an innate ability to remain hopeful in what I could not see with the naked eye. When you're a child, so much of your dreams depend on faith in the unknown. When you go through traumatic events, you can see further down the road.
>
> I believed, hoped, dreamed, and was determined that everything would be all right. I don't pretend to understand the true essence of faith, but I can envision what many people do not see.
>
> One of my professors told me, "You are destined for greatness." I don't know about greatness, but I understand I have a purpose and a destiny. They are written across my life.

In youth, we don't look backward, and our vision of the future isn't clouded by past mistakes or disappointments. As we grow older, our vision of our future narrows. An adult myopia takes hold—a near-sightedness that lets the day-to-day clutter of anxiety and aggravation obscure the big picture. It's hard to see past the mortgage bills, the politics at work, the tensions at home. My most reliable remedy for this disorder is hanging around with kids, listening to their dreams for the future, and remembering my own.

"WHAT WILL BECOME OF FRED?" THAT'S THE QUESTION that echoed through my home when I was a child. I was the son of two accomplished professionals, and my older brother was a good student who seemed destined to follow in my father's footsteps as a doctor.

Meanwhile, I was in second grade and still hadn't learned to read. The letters just never seemed to line up in a comprehensible pattern. I couldn't spell either. One of my earliest and most painful classroom memories is of standing at the blackboard, writing out the spelling words for the week. Behind me I heard my classmates snickering into their hands, then laughing out loud. When I finished writing I couldn't get up the nerve to turn around and face my tormentors. Finally, my teacher blurted out, "Fred, all your *e*'s are backward!"

If anyone had known enough to test me, or known what to test for, they might have diagnosed me as dyslexic. But in the early 1950s, learning disabilities weren't understood, so everyone just thought I was stupid. I also probably had attention deficit disorder, though no one then knew what ADD was either. I couldn't sit still. I was bored and restless, daydreaming my way from one recess to the next. Anything to escape the Chinese water torture of the classroom. I was Louis Pasteur, delivering my Noble Prize speech to the deafening applause of a standing-room-only crowd in Stockholm. . . . I was the pilot of a P-47 Mustang fighter dive-bombing out of the sun toward a Luftwaffe squadron. . . . I was Captain Video, scientific genius and inventor of the Cosmic Ray Vibrator and the Optical Scillometer. "I will neither ask nor give quarter to the forces of evil!" I cried, as I single-handedly saved the world from my fiendish adversary, Dr. Paulie. . . .

I could keep this up for hours, or at least until my teacher, Mrs. Worth, would interrupt my reverie. "Earth to Fred," she'd say, eliciting giggles from my classmates. "Come in, Fred."

Things weren't much better on the home front. I had kind and loving parents, but they had high academic expectations for their sons, and I felt I was disappointing them with every lousy report card. It was a high-powered household, filled with artists and intellectuals, political debate and witty repartee— and I simply couldn't keep up. "What will become of Fred?" the voices whispered. "With luck and hard work he'll get through school, but he'll never get into college."

I had other ideas. By the age of seven, I had fixed on my life's goal—to become a doctor. I wanted to heal the world of all its pain. When I confided my dream to adults, they laughed. "Let's just worry about tonight's homework, Fred.

Then we'll talk about saving the world." But I was convinced that I had what it took, even though no one else seemed to. I've always been an optimist. Maybe I'm just wired that way, or maybe it's an adaptive survival mechanism. In any case, I was determined to become a doctor—and nothing was going to stand in my way.

But first I had to learn to read.

Luckily, my mother's sister, Aunt Lottie, saw how I was struggling and offered to tutor me. She was a schoolteacher and, unlike my other teachers, she was endlessly patient and encouraging. It didn't happen overnight, but gradually the alphabet stopped looking like a foreign language. Then my fifth-grade teacher, Mr. Murphy, tried to figure out why I was failing every written test. He discovered that I could get A's if he tested me orally. For the first time, I felt a glimmer of self-confidence in a classroom.

Now, after raising five kids of my own and being active on the boards of special education programs for years, I'm still impressed by how receptive and responsive children are to positive reinforcement. If you tell children that their future is limitless, and you give them enough love and encouragement, they'll believe you. And they'll believe in themselves. They'll form an inner vision of themselves that they can grow into.

Sadly, children are equally suggestible to negative messages. When I was knocking myself out learning to read, it never occurred to me that there was a smart kid inside fighting to get out. If everyone else could read and write better than I could, then I figured that all the people who thought I was stupid must be right. I'd just have to work twice as hard as the smart kids to get ahead.

High school and college were rough, and my grades were never better than mediocre, but I never lost sight of my goal. I applied to a dozen medical schools and was turned down by all of them. When the dean of NYU told me to my face, "You don't belong in medical school," it only hardened my resolve to prove him wrong. My father saw how determined I was to become a doctor, and he became my advocate. If he hadn't, I probably never would have gotten into medical school. He knew someone who knew someone at New York Medical College, and after a concerted lobbying campaign, they decided to take a chance and admit me.

Once I started medical school, learning was a lot easier. Human anatomy made sense to me in a way that letters and numbers never did. I was good at memorization, which is helpful when you have to learn the names of hundreds of bones, muscles, nerves, and blood vessels—many of them in Latin. For the first time in my life, I felt like a good student. I didn't feel smart—I simply felt like someone who was finally studying something that made sense.

Twenty years later, after I'd become a professor of neurosurgery and director of the pediatric neurosurgical service at NYU, I still thought of myself as an overachiever who was making my mark *despite* my limited intelligence. Then my twelve-year-old daughter, Ilana, started having trouble in school. An educational specialist tested her, and then briefed Kathy and me on her diagnosis. I'll never forget sitting there listening to the specialist describe Ilana's learning disabilities: "Despite a high IQ she has problems with auditory processing, sequencing written commands, reading comprehension."

"But you're describing me!" I blurted out. It was the most dramatic moment of self-revelation I've ever experienced. I felt like the scarecrow at the end of *The Wizard of Oz,* when the Wizard awards him a diploma. I did have a brain! I wasn't stupid; my brain was simply wired to learn differently. So much of the shame I'd been carrying around with me—the mantle of the dumb kid in a smart family, the classroom dunce and butt of cruel jokes—fell away in the instant that I realized I had been struggling all my life with learning disabilities, rather than with limited intelligence. At the age of forty, my view of myself opened up like an automatic convertible cover, blue sky overhead for the first time in my life.

NO MATTER HOW FAR MY EARLY CLASSROOM HUMILIATIONS receded into the past, they continued to hurt in ways that never fully healed. There's a truism about people who end up in the healing professions—that they tend to have a hole in their bucket that they're trying to patch. Though I have a healthy ego, and never lacked self-confidence as a surgeon, I also had a chip on my shoulder. I was driven to be the best at what I did, if only to show up people like that medical school dean. At the same time, I remained highly sensitized to kids—both their suffering and their aspirations for their future. So it's not surprising that even before I got my medical degree, I found myself gravitating toward pediatric patients.

At first I planned to train as a psychiatrist, like my father. But after a neurosurgery rotation my third year in medical school, I was hooked. My neurosurgical mentor at NYU, Joe Ransohoff, warned me, "Being a brain surgeon isn't like being a shrink. A shrink just thinks he's inside a patient's head, but a brain surgeon really is." To me, that was the main appeal of neurosurgery. You could solve serious problems with your bare hands and your intellect. You could actually save kids' lives!

A lot of surgeons are accused of having a God complex. I had a deep-seated superhero complex. Brain tumors in children were evil incarnate to me, and I vowed to wage a personal crusade to defeat them. I admit it sounds grandiose and a bit ridiculous, but that's how I always felt about it. I simply couldn't accept the idea of children dying. I still can't. Tumors in children's brains always filled me with anger. And hearing other surgeons write off whole categories of young tumor patients as "terminal" or "inoperable" sent me into a rage.

So I dedicated myself to going after brain and spinal cord

tumors that other surgeons avoided as too risky. Too risky for whom? The surgeon who wanted to protect his batting average? Losing a patient on the operating table is the hardest part of being a surgeon. But standing by and doing nothing while a child dies was not an option for me. I resolved never to give up on a kid without fighting for as long and hard as the child and his parents were willing.

I became the pediatric neurosurgeon of lost causes. I took on the cases that no one else wanted to touch, particularly children with what were then considered inoperable tumors. I had plenty of bright ideas about how to rescue these hopeless cases. The only problem was that my ideas weren't working. It was a lonely and depressing path. Dr. Ransohoff gave me a lot of encouragement, but few of my other colleagues did.

The challenge was obvious: How do you remove lethal tumors from the brain stem and spinal cord without doing unintended harm to your patients? The solution was elusive, and mistakes never went away. Not for my patients, and not for me. I can remember every case that ever went bad in agonizing detail. I have vivid and precise recall of how and when they went bad, what it looked liked, and most of all, what it felt like.

Marco was a fourteen-year-old boy from northern Italy who came to NYU with a spinal cord tumor. The surgery I performed saved his life, but it left him quadriplegic. Paralysis is always a risk when you operate in the spinal cord. You say it out loud to the patient's family, and they sign a release affirming that they understand the risks. But nobody, including the surgeon, is prepared for that kind of outcome. To this day, I can remember exactly what Marco's feet looked like, because every day for weeks after his surgery I poked and prodded his soles, hoping, begging, and praying for a response that never came. And I remember how those weeks ravaged Marco's father, as his hope ebbed away day by day.

Late one night in the middle of that hellish episode, I sat with Dr. Ransohoff in his office, feeling miserable and hoping he'd say something reassuring. "I don't ever want to go through this again," I said. "You will," he replied.

The horror of failure helped drive me to find a solution. There had to be a way. My father, who was a trailblazer in psychiatry, always told me as a kid, "If you let your mind float free, the ideas will come." After years of having to figure out alternative ways to learn in school, letting my mind float free eventually became second nature. My first surgical breakthrough happened during one of my frequent mind-floats. It wasn't a big "Eureka!" moment. I simply connected some dots in a sequence that, in retrospect, should have been obvious.

It was 1980 and the cool new tool in neurosurgery was the Cavitron, a fine-tipped ultrasonic wand that vibrated 26,000 times a second and liquefied whatever tissue it came into contact with. The Cavitron was being used by a handful of neurosurgeons to liquefy and suction out tumors in locations where a small miscue didn't result in devastating brain damage. I suddenly had a vision of how to use the Cavitron to precisely and harmlessly destroy tumors in the spinal cord. If it worked, we could get beyond "tumor management," which was really just a euphemism for holding actions like radiation. We could actually go for a cure.

As soon as I had the idea, I was convinced it would work. But my colleagues were dubious. "You've got to be kidding, Fred," was one surgeon's response. "You could suck out the whole cord!" Others in our department urged me to experiment with the procedure on a series of laboratory animals. But we had a waiting list of kids who were desperate. I felt I had two choices: to stand by and watch them die, or to try a new approach that I believed could work.

Ransohoff gave me the green light, and so did the parents of a little boy named Steven Benson. Chemotherapy hadn't worked for him, and because of his young age he was too vulnerable to the growth-retarding effects of radiation. He'd simply run out of options. Luckily, the Cavitron worked as I'd envisioned it, and the operation was a success. Steven made a full recovery.

After a dozen successful tumor resections inside the spinal cord, I started publishing my results. Initially, there was some skepticism among surgeons who had been trained in the belief that spinal cord tumors were inoperable. You see the same prejudice today among some neurologists and surgeons who can't believe the quite convincing evidence of occasional spinal cord regeneration among paralyzed patients. Within a year, I had twelve survivors. Eventually there were hundreds. The accumulation of successful outcomes became irrefutable. A few surgeons in other centers began adopting and refining the procedures I'd introduced. As the surgical community gradually got on board, the prognosis for the whole category of pediatric spinal cord tumors was upgraded from terminal to survivable.

EVERY KID IS A PRICELESS SAVE, BUT SOME ARE MORE memorable than others. One of my first—and I have to admit, favorite—spinal cord patients was a boy named Julian Thurston. Julian was from a working-class family in Eastbourne, a city in the south of England, where spinal cord surgery was still considered a medical impossibility. (Even today it's only performed at about a dozen medical centers in the world.)

After Julian was diagnosed with an extremely large spinal cord tumor, his mother, Jane, took him to the leading hospital in London to be examined by the chief of neurosurgery. He concluded that the tumor was inoperable and would soon paralyze and kill Julian. "Your son has only six weeks to live," he said gravely, "Take him home and try to make him comfortable."

Jane Thurston was not a worldly woman, and she wasn't in

the habit of contradicting doctors. But she resolutely refused to accept a death sentence for her eight-year-old son. When a friend of Jane's read an article in *Readers' Digest* about the surgery I was performing at NYU, Jane returned to London and showed the article to the neurosurgical chief. "You know how these Americans are," he said. "Always grandstanding. There's nothing to be done." Luckily, a younger, more open-minded surgeon was in the room at the time, and he agreed to send Julian's CT scans to me at NYU.

When I saw his films, I was confident I could operate on Julian. I urged Jane Thurston to bring him to New York as soon as possible. He was already suffering from significant nerve damage, and I was afraid that if we didn't act quickly he could become fully paralyzed.

I fell for Julian as soon as we met. He was irresistible: a wide-eyed and gentle boy who bubbled over with enthusiasm for his twin passions, sports and the violin. The operation took more than eight hours. Millimeter by millimeter I worked my way down his spine with the Cavitron, destroying the foot-long tumor that lay nestled inside his spinal cord like lead inside a pencil. No mistakes. Julian wiggled all his fingers and toes for me in the recovery room, and the pathology report confirmed that the tumor was benign.

The New York media heard about Julian, and he became an overnight celebrity. Soon the walls of his hospital room were plastered with get-well cards from thousands of New

York kids. My daughter Ilana was the same age as Julian. When he admired her handheld PacMan, she gave it to him, and he was immediately hooked. When a newspaper reporter asked what he missed from England, Julian replied, "My favorite breakfast cereal, Weetabix." The story traveled across the Atlantic, and two days later a huge crate of Weetabix arrived by air freight from the manufacturer in England.

When the New York Metropolitan Taxi Board of Trade found out that Julian's father was a cabbie back in England, they donated the money to fly him and Julian's sister over for a post-op family reunion. Meanwhile, back in Eastbourne, the Thurstons' neighbors were staging a benefit spelling bee to raise money to cover Julian's hospital expenses. Ten days after his operation, Julian and his family went home.

Julian made a good recovery, but he was no longer able to excel at his first love, sports. Before his operation, he'd been one of the best all-round athletes in his class, the star of the soccer team, and the fastest sprinter in the school. After his surgery and rehab, he was only average. So he took up music—a turning point that opened up new worlds to him. He practiced the violin three hours a day and earned a music scholarship to a top-flight private school his family would never have been able to afford. He got a great education, continued to excel at music, and, at the age of sixteen, became the youngest violinist in the Eastbourne Symphony Orchestra. That same year Julian returned to NYU to give a concert for the patients and medical staff. It was one of those days that being a neurosurgeon felt like the best job in the world.

Julian went on to college, and played with the Kensington Symphony into his mid-twenties. Today, at twenty-eight, he lives in London where he's a lawyer for one of England's leading media companies. He plays squash and soccer—and the violin. "My girlfriend would probably describe me as 'driven,'" he says with a laugh. "But I just think of myself as directed. I see my life moving forward, from strength to strength. If there's something I want to do, I don't agonize over it. I learned earlier than most people that you only get one go-round, so I'm determined to make the most of it."

AS MANY MORE OF MY "TERMINAL" PATIENTS SURVIVED, I began noticing something even more remarkable than their medical recoveries. It was the way kids like Julian, who had been written off for dead, got back to the business of living. They didn't return to their lives unscathed or undiminished. Many of them carried physical scars and neurological deficits of varying degrees, and the emotional wounds they suffered were even more punishing. But somehow these kids emerged from their medical crises with a clearer sense of purpose and newfound reserves of strength. Having encountered the fragility of life firsthand, they understood just how precious a gift life is. Going forward, every day counted for them, and for their families. No week was ever again ordinary or boring. No friendship was ever taken for granted.

I've come to think of Julian's statement—"You only get one go-round, so you better make the most of it"—as the "outlier's creed." In any statistical analysis of a group, there is a certain small percentage of people who defy the odds, whose outcome falls altogether outside the bell curve of expected results. These anomalous individuals are called outliers.

I know something about being an outlier. The odds of my ever making it to medical school were very steep. And no one, including myself, would have guessed that I'd actually go on to have a notable career as a surgeon. More recently, emerging from a monthlong coma while in my sixties and making a good recovery cast me once again as a statistical outlier.

But my qualifications as an outlier are dwarfed by the odds many of my pediatric patients have overcome just to survive—not to mention the adversity they've had to face in rebuilding their lives. Imagine showing up for the first day of eighth grade with a surgical scar running down the back of your shaved head. Imagine trying to measure up to this season's standard of cool when the left side of your face droops when you smile.

These children are off the curve because they have not only survived diseases that would have been fatal a decade earlier—they have thrived. They have excelled at school, launched careers and families, and made significant contributions to their communities. They have rebuilt their lives and inspired the people whose lives they have touched.

Like many returning war veterans, these kids have had to struggle to reassimilate themselves into peer groups whose day-to-day preoccupations with money and clothes and social status now seem trivial. As desperately as they want to simply blend in and return to a "normal" life, they will always stand apart, forever transformed by their experiences.

The life force burns with added intensity in these young people. What they see on the road ahead of them is a series of precious daily opportunities: to connect with other people in a meaningful way, to extend a helping hand to others who are struggling to survive, to make a contribution to their community, to simply smell the flowers and count their blessings.

I've watched with a mixture of pride and amazement as these young people have plunged back into their lives. In June I get graduation announcements and wedding invitations. At Christmas I get cards updating me on their growing careers and families. They haven't all lived happily ever after. Sometimes I've seen them again as patients when tumors grew back. Too often I've gone to their funerals and wakes. But whatever the span of their days, they remained fighters. They've become my heroes and my role models.

Chelsea Snyder is an outlier in every sense of the word. When she was diagnosed with a rare kind of brain tumor at the age of six, her doctors in Wisconsin gave her mother,

Lucina, a grim prognosis: *No one with Chelsea's disease has ever survived.* They operated on her the first day of first grade, and she did well. Six years later, her tumor reappeared in her brain stem, and her doctors told her there was nothing more they could do. They gave her three months to live.

Lucina didn't think so. "I just couldn't accept that or even consider letting go at this point. Something within me said, *It's not time to give up.* I was ready to take her anywhere and try anything." She scoured medical journals and the Internet until she found out about our hospital. Then she worked with a nonprofit group called Angel Flight to fly Chelsea and herself to New York to see me. "I didn't know when we left for New York if I would return with my daughter alive or in a coffin," says Lucina. "The fear, the unknowing were unbearable. Chelsea was so strong through it all. She believed that if she was going to die the doctors would use her case to help find a cure for her disease and save other children. This, from a thirteen-year-old! I tried to draw on her strength and ideals, and at least give the illusion that I was strong for her sake."

I operated on Chelsea and she rebounded very quickly. She was walking the halls of the hospital the day after surgery, and insisting to anyone who'd listen that she wasn't leaving town until she did some sight-seeing. Two weeks later, after a three-day whirlwind tour of Manhattan, she ran down the hall to my office shouting, "I *love* New York!"

Today, Chelsea is a seventeen-year-old who gets A's and B's

in high school. I can't guarantee that she'll never have another recurrence, but she isn't waiting for a clean bill of health to get on with her life. She has a job at the mall, she has a boyfriend, and she has her own car. She's organized a youth cancer support group through her local hospitals, and she participates every year in the local benefit walk for cancer research. She's planning to become a pediatric nurse and work with children in an oncology ward.

Meanwhile, Chelsea's mother has taken inspiration from her daughter's ability to look to the future despite the unknowns that persist. "I too have made plans," Lucina reports proudly. "At the ripe old age of forty-three, I am finally a college student! I'm studying for a degree in counseling, so I can work with other families of cancer patients."

As much as she'd like to have a normal teenager's life, Chelsea has learned to adapt to her differences, both internal and external. One of her eyes only opens partway ("I'm always playing around with makeup to make it less noticeable"), and her smile is a little crooked from latent facial paralysis ("I figure if people can't handle it, it's their problem"). She has no patience with people who sweat the small stuff. "It's annoying to me how other kids complain about little things. I mean really, what's the big deal if you get a C on a test, or your boyfriend doesn't call you after school?"

Most of all, she has had to cope with the specter of her disease, which she understands may still overtake her plans for the future. "I've thought about death a lot. Who wouldn't in my situation? I just try to take things a day at a time. Because of my experience I have become a very strong young woman. I've learned to plan for my future and enjoy the present along the way. You do what you can when you can. I tried to give blood last month, but the blood bank wouldn't take it because of the medication I'm on. So instead I registered to become an organ donor. If I die, I figure someone else will need my heart or my kidneys to survive. Death is part of life, but I can't worry about when or how. I've got too many plans."

Making plans—particularly in the face of daunting odds—is one of life's boldest acts. For outliers, making the big plan, dreaming the big dream, is where every day begins.

I'VE MET MOST OF MY PATIENTS FOR THE FIRST TIME VIA two-dimensional transparencies of their brain or spinal column. In a typical week twenty or more sets of films would arrive at my office from far-flung locales. My assistant would pile them on my desk or clip them up on my light box for review. The pictures we get these days of the inside of a patient's head or spine are remarkably revealing; but this wasn't always the case.

So much of the history of neurosurgery has been a cat-and-mouse game between imaging technologies and elusive tumors nestled deep inside the brain and spinal cord. Over the course of my career, imaging has become progressively more insightful and less invasive. When I started out as a neurosurgeon we only had specialized X rays that required injections—either of air into the brain or iodine into the arteries to light up the tumor. In the '70s we got CT scans, which were less invasive and more precise at locating tumors. In the '80s, MRIs gave us even sharper pictures of the spinal cord, nerves, and brain. The '90s brought positron emission tomography (PET scans) and MRI spectroscopy, which show us the metabolism and growth rate of a tumor. Today we even have functional MRIs that light up the neural pathways of speech and movement.

But despite all these advances in imaging, the brain is still the most mysterious organ in the body. It's a classic case of "the more you know, the more you know you don't know." When you peer into the brain through our current high-tech window, you see a system of neural pathways so complex that it will take another century to map them. It's like the Hubble telescope. Perched above Earth's atmosphere, it can see farther into space than we could ever imagine—and it reveals a universe that is vaster and more trackless than we'll ever be able to explore.

All our smart technology doesn't make the true nature of the brain any more transparent. We still don't know what most of the brain does, or how it does it. And we don't know why tumors grow there. We know which parts of the brain feel pain or fear or joy, but not how they manufacture emotions out of neurotransmitters, enzymes, and endorphins.

I've always believed in treating patients, not images. Meeting and examining the patient in person fills in the missing human dimension. I usually feel as if I've already met my patients when they first come into my office. There's a magical inside-out moment when the brain scan I've reviewed merges with the face of the young person sitting across from me on my couch. During our conversation and the physical exam that follows, what I think of as the patient's fourth dimension comes into focus. I don't call it their aura—I'm not that New Age. It's my holistic perception as a physician of where my patient hurts and where he or she is whole.

When you actually meet the tumor during surgery, a different kind of vision guides you—the intuition and experience to know when to be aggressive and when to be cautious, when to move forward and when to retreat. No matter what kind of high-tech scalpel you have in your hand—whether it's a Gamma Knife with focused cobalt radiation or an endoscope connected to a fiber-optic camera—your most important tool as a surgeon is always your judgment.

Outside the OR, so much depends on refining and enlarging your sense of vision—both your inner vision of what's most important to you, and your outer vision of the world around you. If you want to get anywhere in life, you have to see who you are and where you're going. So many things are unavoidably random and beyond your control—the family you're born into, who you meet and fall in love with, all the accidents of time and place, both happy and sad. But you *can* control the direction of your life—if you have a destination to hold firmly in your sights.

You also need to have a vision if you want to lead, whether you're in politics, business, or even medicine. If you have a clear vision you can articulate, people will follow you—because everyone wants a piece of a vision. We all do. Otherwise we're just stumbling around in the dark, hoping not to collide with something hard and sharp. When I launched the INN, I didn't try to persuade anyone to come with me. I simply described what I envisioned—a healing environment built around human needs and human talent, rather than mere technology—and a lot of people decided it was a vision they wanted to help breathe life into. That's how fantasies become real: a group of people seize on the same vision and make it their own.

FANTASY IS A MOTIVATIONAL TECHNIQUE WE ALL USE TO get from point A to dimly perceived point B. Virtually all Academy Award winners confess to first rehearsing their acceptance speech in their living room as a ten-year-old. Of course, there are thousands of would-be movie stars who never make it onto the silver screen, but that doesn't mean they dreamed in vain. For many of us, fantasizing is how we subordinate our fears to our hopes.

For children, making believe is second nature. They can

don a bath towel and become a superhero. They can migrate effortlessly between cowboys and Indians, princesses and evil witches. For the kids I meet who are fighting for their lives, fantasy is an irreplaceable weapon in their arsenal.

Matthew Brodie, a four-year-old patient of mine, had to endure several surgeries and a lot of physical pain in his young life due to a tumor in his lower spinal chord. He became a master at using fantasy to keep his fears at bay.

"You're a cod fish, Smee!" cried Matthew, as he held up his little plastic hook and waved it menacingly at his mother who sat perched on the edge of his hospital bed. A pirate hat and painted mustache completed the fantasy and for a few moments he forgot about the tubes and wires that ran off his little body.

When imagination was being handed out, Matthew got in line twice. He loved to pretend, as so many children do. His greatest passion was superheroes and each morning—after strapping braces onto his legs—he'd pull open the bottom drawer of his dresser, which was stuffed with costumes. "So, who are we today?" his mother would ask him. Pawing through the garments, he would yank out a black satin cape and shout, "Zorro!" Off to the grocery store they would go in black boots, tasseled hat, pencil-thin mustache, and the cape trailing behind.

Matthew's need to become fictional characters was a constant preoccupation and many people found it rather odd and eccentric. But it was actually a brilliant way for his young psyche to handle all the frightening and painful experiences that he had to face. The night before returning to the hospital for a third spinal operation, Matthew was seized with fear. As his mother tucked him into bed, he whispered into her ear, "Maybe I could go as Batman." For months, Matthew had begged her to buy him the full Batman outfit that he'd seen in the window of the local costume shop. It was very expensive and she had always turned him down. That night she relented, and the next morning they stopped by the costume store before heading to the hospital.

Matthew made the long trip into the city with the Batman costume tucked tightly under his arm. He and his mother huddled next to the car in the parking garage and put it all on before entering the hospital. The finishing touch was the hood that completely covered Matthew's face in a cocoon of super strength. Fully arrayed, Batman sauntered down the sidewalk while his mother followed a few steps behind him with tears blurring her vision. He strutted up through the hospital doors very proudly with all the composure that Batman unfailingly maintains. The bustling hall of the hospital was filled with people and many called out, "Hey, Batman!" as he passed. Very coolly, he raised a hand and acknowledged them silently. Batman rarely speaks, you know. He marched into his last operation without a qualm. After all, he was the all-powerful Caped Crusader.

That final operation did the trick. Matthew is now fourteen years old and has only minor deficits. His costumes became less and less necessary as the pain of the ordeal faded. But I guess he hasn't totally given up on the superhero concept, since he's now a first-degree black belt in Tae Kwon Do.

In addition to heightened imagination, children have the advantage of innocence. They believe that growing up can transform them into different, better people. The future is a place of endless possibilities for children.

Adults tend to learn a different lesson as we grow older—that our identity is gradually hardening into a form-fitting shell that defines who we are, what we believe, and what we can accomplish. And that's the trap we all have to avoid, because once we believe we're as grown up as we'll ever get, it's Game Over.

As we age, we tend to forget the liberating power of fantasies. We certainly become more secretive about them. We don't want to be seen as a Walter Mitty, endlessly daydreaming about adventure, romance, money. But down deep, we're all Walter Mitty. Who doesn't like to imagine himself smarter, handsomer, braver?

I'm a firm believer in the power of positive fantasy, at every stage of life. Fantasies don't have to be grandiose to be therapeutic. They're worthwhile if they simply put a smile on your face in the middle of a stressful day. At their best, they let you believe in yourself unconditionally. That's what make-believe is all about: believing in something you want to create or in someone you want to become, if only for few moments a day.

Anyone who visits my office at the hospital gets a pretty good idea of my ongoing fantasy life. On the windowsill you'll see an antique model car. I have this thing for old cars—maybe it has to do with growing up in the fifties. I know they're just metal and paint, but if you've ever sat behind the wheel of a 1959 Cadillac Eldorado convertible, you understand what it feels like to time-travel.

The walls of my office are adorned with old-time baseball memorabilia. I've found they make for friendlier decorations than the usual medical diplomas and certificates, particularly when my visitors are sitting down to talk about a tumor in their child's head. Showing a kid and his father an autographed photo of Lou Gerhig and explaining what made his swing so fearsome takes some of the edge off the harsh topic of the moment. For me, the soul of baseball has always been rooted in fantasy. No matter what I might accomplish in the OR, I'm never going to pitch the seventh game of the World Series. But I can dream. . . .

My sofa and chairs are strewn with pillows of storybook characters that my wife has needlepointed. One of my favorite characters is Peter Pan, who's something of a patron saint to me. Maybe I just never grew up, but if you ask me, Peter Pan has gotten a bad rap. Pop psychologists have had a field day running roughshod over him, remaking him into an icon of narcissism and immaturity. I plead guilty to all of the sins attributed to Peter Pan. I don't want to grow up—not if it means growing old and giving up daydreams. I don't want to go to school—I never did have much fun there. I don't want to follow rules. And yes, I know the way to Neverland— "Second star to the right, straight on till morning."

3

Face Your Fears

Courage is not the absence of fear, but rather the
judgment that something else is more important than fear.

—Ambrose Redmoon

We're hardwired to feel fear; it's our oldest evolutionary adaptation. When a saber-toothed tiger charged at us from out of the brush, we instinctively fled for our lives. If the tiger went after our child or our mate, we might have decided to stand and fight.

It's called the flight-or-fight response—part reflex, part choice. Though we've subdued most of our natural predators, modern life has its own cast of saber-tooths that strike fear in our hearts and confront us with flight-or-fight choices. We fear failure. We fear pain. We fear loss—of love, of money, of status, of youth. Most of all, we fear death.

Fear is an inescapable part of being alive. What counts is whether or not we let our fears keep us from engaging the toughest challenges or pursuing our most cherished goals. We each fight these battles every day—between our fear of failure and our desire for achievement, between our fear of intimacy and our desire for connection, between our fear of looking foolish and our drive to transcend our limits. We can all look back on our lives and see opportunities that we let get away—in work, in love, in friendships and families—because we lost our nerve.

So many people—often the most intelligent and talented professionals—never achieve their most cherished goals because they're afraid to fail. I've known many terrifically talented surgeons who have been hamstrung by their fear of failure. They shy away from the most difficult cases because they get attached to their success rate, which they wear like a badge of honor. It's natural not to want to fail. The stakes are so high, for patients and surgeons alike, and there's so little margin for error. But when fear wins out over courage, everyone loses. I've seen brilliant physicians balk at pursuing new, potentially lifesaving ideas for fear of looking foolish if their new idea fails—as most new ideas do.

When I was a boy, my father framed the cost benefit of risk-taking this way: "You've got to be willing to look like a jackass if you're ever going to look like a genius." At the time, I was feeling like a jackass on a daily basis in school. An unwilling jackass to be sure, but I understood that if I let myself be ruled by my fear of looking foolish, I would never learn to learn. Once I figured out that no one believed I'd ever get to college, much less medical school, I decided I'd just have to bull my way forward if I ever hoped to get there. So I lowered my head and pushed against my fear of failure—which fortunately collapsed from exhaustion before I did. By the time I got to high school, I had failed so often for so long that I'd become inured to it.

Along the way, I figured out the most important lesson of my life: *Once you stop fearing failure, you're free.* You can go after any crazy idea you can dream up. Everything becomes possible when there's nothing you're afraid to try.

When I became a surgeon, I was always willing to explore any idea that held promise. I embraced Thomas Edison's credo: "I haven't failed, I've found 10,000 ways that don't work." Nineteen new ideas out of twenty were likely to be wrongheaded. But the twentieth one might save a child's life, and many more children thereafter. By my math, the price of doing nothing was always greater than the cost of risking failure. I went down dozens of blind alleys. I kept trying new approaches, and eventually, one of them worked.

In my years as a surgeon, I've had a close-up view of what people can achieve when they face their worst fears. Inside a crucible of pain, both physical and emotional, I've seen the base metals of human nature transformed into gold. One of the most courageous people I've worked with is a thirteen-year-old patient of mine named Spenser Scharfman. Spenser has spent virtually his entire young life battling a brain stem tumor that keeps growing back.

Last August Spenser performed his bar mitzvah before a standing-room-only crowd at his family's synagogue. His brother and father rolled his wheelchair up a ramp onto the altar, and they supported him as he stood to read from the Torah. Though his larynx was partially obstructed by a recent tracheotomy, he spoke clearly and forcefully about what this coming-of-age ceremony meant to him: "A bar mitzvah is important to me because it is another step to becoming a man, to meeting the challenges and overcoming the obstacles in life."

In a recent letter, Spenser gave me a little glimpse at what's kept him fighting for the eleven years since he was first diagnosed with a brain stem tumor.

> Dear Dr. Fred,
>
> Love is inside me and it keeps me going. This tumor has never stopped me and it never will. Even though I have a crazy life and I have mixed emotions about it every day and think it sucks like hell, I also have all these nurses and doctors and machines that help me physical-wise and a huge enormous team of sweet loving and caring people including a brother, 2 dogs, a snake, 2 turtles and a suitcase full of cousins and friends that are like my best pals in the whole wide world.
>
> This crappy tumor really sucks! I mean, like how many MRIs can a kid take? I still get angry and upset a lot, but I have the courage to get better whether it's next week or a year from now. No matter when it is

that the day of the miracle in everyone's life comes,
it will happen.
   To miracles!
Spenser

This is a kid who never got to do what other boys were doing. He couldn't walk, much less run and kick a ball. He's never had the chance to fit in. Many adults would flee in terror and self-pity from the hand Spenser has been dealt. He chooses to stand and fight—not simply to endure, but to prevail.

To flee or to fight, to submit or to overcome—that remains the eternal and recurring choice. No matter how many situations we shy away from in fear, new ones surface daily. That's where we test our metal—in the everyday challenges to do whatever is toughest. Every circumstance is different, but the summons to our courage remains the same:

Embrace what's scariest.

Understand that the reward usually outweighs the risk.

Remember that our best self is our most courageous self.

FACING FEAR IS AN ONGOING CHALLENGE. NO MATTER how long you wrestle with it, fear never goes away. I've often felt it ripple through my chest when I've entered a sick child's room—fear that I wouldn't be able to make his pain go away, fear that a parent would ask me to perform a medical miracle that I couldn't deliver. I've finally come to accept that courage isn't the absence of fear, or even the mastery of fear. It's refusing to let fear master you.

In the OR, a healthy respect for fear is a necessity. As a surgeon, you have to go into every operation believing that you can save your patient, and with the self-confidence to believe that you're the person for the job. But you also know from experience how many ways things can go bad. And how quickly.

Neurosurgery can be described as three hours of hard work and thirty minutes of terror—the thirty minutes when you come face-to-face with the tumor you've been imaging on film and in your mind for days. The terror is always there, no matter how many operations you've performed. It's a fear you have to subdue before you can lift the scalpel and make the first incision. But you learn that fear is also your ally in the OR. It keeps you humble, and it keeps you from getting complacent or careless.

During a long operation, you have to remain both vigilant and relaxed. It's an agonizing kind of tension, but if you let the agony overwhelm you, you'll screw up. You have to stay relaxed, so when the pit of pure terror opens up at your feet, you don't fall in.

One of my worst scares in the OR came during a case that began like a fairy tale. Luis Olmedo was an Equadorian Indian who grew up in a dirt-floor shack in one of Guayaquil's worst slums. At the age of six, he developed severe pain along his spinal axis. When the local herbalist couldn't make the pain go away, Luis's mother wrapped him in a shawl and carried him to the cathedral to pray to the Holy Virgin for guidance. Walking home, she passed in front of a World Health Organization clinic and decided to take Luis inside. As it happens, the clinic was run by one of my former residents, Don Brickelmeyer, who diagnosed Luis's spinal cord tumor. Within a week of Don's phone call to me, we'd arranged to have Luis and his mother flown up to NYU. We had a fund at the hospital for special-needs cases like Luis's, and Don was able to help at his end with the passports and visas.

Luis's spinal tumor was more complicated than Julian Thurston's had been because it was interwoven with the tissue inside the cord. We'd continued to refine our techniques in the six years since Julian's surgery, so I was confident I could remove it. Luis's mother explained to him that the Virgin Mary had led them here to New York, where the doctors had more powerful magic than the healers back home. What we had, in fact, was every piece of state-of-the-art med-tech wizardry you could cram into an OR, plus a crack team of experienced surgical specialists. What we needed was a little bit of luck.

Luis arrived in the OR clutching a teddy bear. After we anesthetized Luis, the head nurse sent the teddy bear ahead to the recovery room. First we made a long incision down a length of his vertebrae. Then we cut away the connective tissue that surrounded the spine and inserted retractors to keep it exposed. Next, we used a Bovie electrocautery knife to separate the muscle from the bone. Then, using a compact pneumatic drill called a Midas Rex, we cut out a foot-long section of back bone and lifted it off the spine. Finally, we made our way past the ligaments inside the spine to the dura, the membrane that covers and protects the cord itself.

I placed an ultrasound transducer on the dura, which transmitted pictures of the tumor onto the video screen above the operating table. The tumor was enormous—much larger than it had appeared on the MRIs. Using microscissors under the operating microscope, I cut through the dura, in much the same way you'd slice the casing of a sausage—just a lot more carefully. Underneath all the protective layers of skin, tissue, muscles, bone, ligament, and dura lies the exquisitely fragile spinal cord itself. The best metaphor for the cord is the bundles of fiber-optic strands inside the cables that transmit phones signals. But these nerve pathways are so tiny that to the naked eye the cord has a white, viscous appearance. Even with the ten-times magnification of the operating microscope, it's impossible to distinguish individual nerve pathways, and it was hard to find the boundaries between the white matter and the reddish-gray tumor tissue in Luis's spine. As I'd feared, the tumor had developed its own vascular system, which meant it would bleed into the cord as we resected it.

The trick was to destroy as much of the tumor as possible without doing any damage to the nerve pathways connecting the brain to the rest of the body. Using the Cavitron, I began to gently debulk the tumor and suck it out of the cord. My assisting surgeon followed right behind me with a focus-heat carbon dioxide laser that cauterized the tumor's veins and arteries to control the bleeding.

Two hours after we began, we were barely at the halfway point. "We're getting an irregular heartbeat," the anesthesiologist called out. Seconds later, an alarm bell sounded. Luis's blood pressure collapsed and another alarm went off. For a surgeon, the sound of those alarms in mid-surgery is your worst nightmare. When you're debulking a spinal cord tumor under high magnification, everything proceeds very, very slowly. It's as if you're climbing a steep glacier, planting one painstaking crampon at a time. Then the alarms go off, and everything vaults into fast-forward.

Luis continued to free-fall. His heart went into ventricular fibrillation. "Cardiac arrest in OR ten," the anesthesiologist broadcast over the intercom.

We quickly withdrew the Cavitron and the laser. The nurses swung the operating scope out of the way. I knew I needed to get Luis onto his back and start massaging his heart—but first we had to close up his spinal cord. "Let's pack it," I ordered. We packed the operating field with sponges to soak up the blood, then we covered the wound with towels. Not the ideal dressing for an open spinal cord, but we had to turn him over—right away.

We rotated him as gently as we could, and I began external cardiac massage. I pushed rhythmically against his chest with the flats of my hands, wishing I could press harder but fearful for his exposed spine. The doors to the OR flew open and the emergency team hurried in with the crash cart at the ready. They injected epinephrine directly into Luis's heart, and other drugs into his IVs. Nothing happened.

Someone handed me the defib paddles from the crash cart. They looked huge as I placed them against Luis's tiny chest. "Stand back," I said. "Hit it." Luis's body convulsed under the paddles, but the shock failed to restart his heart. "Crank it up . . . now stand back . . . and hit it." I delivered three more countershocks in succession. Nothing.

I restarted external heart massage to get some blood flowing to his brain. Minutes were ticking by. By now there were fifteen people crowded around the table trying to get this kid back on line, but nothing was working. All the commotion around the table was drowned out by the voice inside my head that was silently shouting to Luis, "Let's go, buddy! Come back to us—now!"

I may have been calling the shots around the table, but I couldn't make Luis's heart start beating. We kept shocking and injecting and massaging his heart, our finely tuned teamwork tap-dancing on the edge of panic. No one was willing to "call" this kid, no matter how long he'd been in arrest.

Twenty-nine minutes after Luis's heart stopped, it started beating again. Don't ask how. When a miracle drops out of the sky and lands in your lap, you don't ask for the return address. Two minutes later his blood pressure had returned to normal.

The crash team gathered their equipment and rolled the cart out of the room. The surgical group stood around the table, totally drained. The first person to speak was a medical student who was observing the operation. "Does this happen often?" he asked. Everyone started to giggle, then to laugh out loud.

When we quieted down, the anesthesiologist spoke up. "Fred, can we please close this kid up now, before he crashes again?"

We were only halfway through our operating plan. When you cut away most of a benign tumor, the remainder will often wither away if it's just a small fragment. But with an interwoven growth like Luis's, what you leave behind will grow back with renewed intensity. Unless we got it all, Luis didn't have a chance.

"We're going to continue," I heard myself reply.

A discussion ensued. The anesthesiologist was adamant. Everyone stood stock-still in their positions during the debate. In the end, it was my call. "Let's turn him," I said. We turned Luis over onto his stomach, unpacked the wound, and flushed it out with antibiotics. Then we went back to work on the tumor.

An hour and a half later we were done. The tumor—or at least anything that was visible under ten-times magnification—

was gone. We backed out very slowly, stitching the dura back up, carefully replacing and reattaching the backbone, suturing the muscle and the skin, and finally dressing the wound. We removed his breathing tube and wheeled him out toward the recovery room.

I had a Spanish-speaking medical student standing at my side when Luis regained consciousness a few minutes later. The rest of the surgical team was crowded behind us in the recovery room. When Luis woke up, he moved each finger and toe on command. Everyone cheered, so he did it again, smiling at our applause.

No paralysis. So far so good. But after a half hour of cardiac arrest, there was still the possibility of brain damage. "Ask him where he is," I directed the medical student, who translated my question.

"Nueva York," Luis replied.

"And who am I?" The student translated my question, and Luis answered.

"He says you are Dr. Epstein, the tall magician," reported the medical student with a smile. "And he wants to know who took his teddy bear."

KEEPING A COOL HEAD IN A CRISIS IS A LOT EASIER WHEN the disaster is happening to someone else. When you wake up to a nightmare in your own life, it's a hell of a lot scarier. If you're a young person with plans and dreams for your future, nothing is more frightening than facing a future where all the ground rules have changed and the goal posts have been moved back fifty yards.

Robin Taylor has a rare genetic disorder called neurofibromatosis II, or NF2, that afflicts only one in every 40,000 people, causing brain tumors that envelop the auditory nerve. So you can't blame Robin for wondering "Why me?" when she was first diagnosed at the age of sixteen.

She bounced back strong from her initial surgery, and radiation helped shrink the tumors we couldn't reach. She finished high school and went off to college hoping for a fresh start. She was only three months into her freshman year when her hearing started to fail. As often happens with NF2, the fibroid tumors had grown back and were pressing against the auditory nerve center in her brain stem. She hired a notetaker to help her record her half-heard classroom lectures, but it was only a holding action. By Christmas, she had to drop out and go home for more treatment.

Robin was depressed and confused. What about the life she'd planned for herself? How could she become a teacher if she couldn't even finish college? Would she ever hear her own children's voices? Would she even be able to have children?

The hardest part of all was losing touch with her friends. They had always hung out together or talked on the phone, discussing whatever they were doing and feeling that day. She lost many of her friends along with her hearing. They had busy lives, and now the only way she could communicate with them was via e-mail. It was scary and lonely. She felt ashamed of the way her body had let her down.

When her father suggested she enroll in a sign-language class, Robin panicked. She'd done enough reading on-line to know that many NF2 patients end up deaf—but not her! She was just having a down cycle in her treatment. Her doctors would figure out what to do next—and then she'd be able to hear again. Learning sign language would be giving up. She might just as well hang a sign around her neck reading I'M DEAF. THROW ME A PEANUT.

Robin does have surgical options. The tumors can be removed, and some NF2 patients have recently been able to recover their hearing through a cochlear electrode implant. But the facial nerves that run right alongside the auditory nerves are often damaged in this type of surgery. "If that happens," Robin writes to me in an e-mail, "I won't be able to smile, cry, move my eyebrows, close my eyes. How would I deal with not being able to smile? I have a smile for everything and for everyone. That's who I am!"

Robin's still thinking about whether or not to go ahead with the surgery. In the meantime, she's made a decision about her education, which she sent me in an e-mail:

> Being so dependent on e-mail made me realize how
> isolated I've become. I'll never get to be a teacher if I
> can't communicate with students. So I've started taking
> signing classes at the local community college. I
> thought I'd hate it, that it would make me feel like a

loser. But there I was in my first class learning to sign my name, and I looked around the room and it was full of people. Deaf people and hearing people. And by the end of the first week I could sign back and forth to all of them! It felt great to be back in school, to be studying and talking with friends again.

WHEN I WAS A TEENAGER IN THE 1950S, I WAS A DIE-HARD Brooklyn Dodgers fan. My baseball gods were Jackie Robinson, Duke Snider, and Gil Hodges. My Valhalla was Ebbets Field.

In 1952, a center fielder for the Boston Red Sox was setting records for bad behavior. Jimmy Piersall was a talented rookie who made as many headlines for his pranks as for his ball playing. He ran the bases backward and hid behind the monuments in Yankee Stadium's center field. At first people just thought of him as the team clown, but as the season wore on his behavior on and off the field became increasingly bizarre. Then, in August, Piersall suffered what used to be called a "nervous breakdown." We were all used to Hollywood starlets having breakdowns, but it was shocking and newsworthy when a jock in a macho sport like baseball ended up in a mental hospital getting shock therapy.

When he came out of the hospital, Piersall battled back to the majors and regained his place on the team. Not that anyone made it easy for him. The '50s weren't the most tolerant or compassionate time when it came to mental illness, particularly among athletes. Baseball fans in opposing ball-parks heckled him mercilessly. Here was a guy recovering from a crippling anxiety disorder, trying to hit a major league fastball with thousands of spectators shouting, "Go back to the loony bin, you whacko!" It didn't take Piersall long to figure out how to shut them up. He went six for six his first game back.

The title of Piersall's 1955 autobiography, and the 1957 movie Hollywood made from it, says it all: *Fear Strikes Out.* He wasn't ashamed of his breakdown. He wanted people to know that you could have a mental illness, get better, and come back to play ball in the big leagues. He was proud to be a different kind of role model. "Probably the best thing that ever happened to me was going nuts," he said near the end of his career. "Whoever heard of Jimmy Piersall, until that happened?"

Piersall had a long and very productive baseball career. He made the All-Star Team twice and was considered by many to be the best fielding center-fielder of his era—better than DiMaggio, better than Mantle. Sandy Koufax, the Dodger fastballer, and a contemporary of Piersall's, defined pitching as "the art of instilling fear." Jimmy Piersall not only faced down the league's scariest pitchers; he triumphed over his inner demons. When fear struck out at Fenway Park, everyone who struggled with their inner demons stood a little taller.

I was one of them. Between the ages of twelve and seventeen, I was battling against depression. I was deeply discouraged and ashamed of my poor performance at school, and I was plagued by doubts that I'd ever be able to achieve my most cherished goal of becoming a doctor. Depression wasn't commonly diagnosed and treated in those days; this was thirty years before Prozac came on the scene and kicked depression out of the closet. Luckily for me, my father was a pioneering psychiatrist who specialized in treating depression. He recognized that I was clinically depressed, and he prescribed the first generation of antidepressants that were just coming into use. He also got me into psychotherapy. They worked. I still struggled in school and had to look for ways to resurrect my self-esteem outside the classroom, but I no longer felt hopeless. Without hope, my dreams for my future would have withered and died.

As a teenager struggling for a sliver of status and recognition, I played to whatever strengths I had at hand. I had a good sense of humor, and I soon discovered that laughter was a valued social currency. I was a good listener; girls, and later women, appreciated this. Having suffered my own share of anguish, I was empathetic. I could tell where other people hurt, which made it easier to gain their trust and friendship. I got a lot of mileage out of anger and denial; I learned to channel my anger into achievement, deny the chorus of doubting voices, and tap into my competitive side when it was most useful to me. I was determined and adaptive. I had to be. If one technique for learning didn't work, I tried something else.

My main sanctuary from adolescent angst was sports. I

loved to compete, and I loved to play baseball and football. When I was twelve and had pretty much hit bottom emotionally, I met Frank Hennessey. Frank had once been a lightweight prizefighter in his youth, though the closest he ever got to a title was being knocked out by 1940s lightweight champion Fido Kempton. By the early 1950s, he was the boxing coach at my prep school in the Bronx, looking for some young talent to train in what's been called the "sweet science" of boxing.

I liked boxing. Maybe it was the "sweet science" of it that appealed to me—finding your way inside an opponent's defenses is a lot like resecting a tumor from deep inside the brain stem. It tests your nerves, your patience, and your poise. And of course there weren't any better outlets for a frustrated teenager than hitting a bag, or better yet, an opponent.

To my mind, the chief value of competition is that it gives you the chance to fail. People think competition is all about winning—but it's really about learning to lose. You learn that it's never as bad as you fear it will be. When you're involved in competitive sports, you figure out what a lot of people who stay on the sidelines never see: that even when you fail, there's always another at-bat, another inning, another game, another opportunity to compete and to win. You don't have to do it all with one swing of the bat.

Competitive sports have been a lifeline for many of my patients, both boys and girls. Even if their bodies aren't perfect, they desperately want to be *in* the game, not on the side-lines.

Roy Emerson was a full-of-beans seven-year-old when I took out a benign tumor that was pressing on his pituitary gland. The next winter he wanted to go skiing. His mother was appalled by the idea, but I explained to her that there was no medical reason he couldn't ski, as long as he wore a helmet. I'll never forget the smile Roy had on his face when he left my office that day.

Roy went on to become a great all-round athlete and a high school football star. He won a full athletic scholarship to Temple University where he got to live out his boyhood dream of playing Division 1A football in the Big East Conference. As a freshman he was already starting as defensive tackle on the varsity team.

His team was having a great season. In late October, they beat the nation's #3-ranked team in front of 65,000 fans. The next week, Roy started to have headaches. He didn't think anything of it at first. Headaches were nothing unusual for a defensive lineman who literally butted heads with other 300-pound players every day. But the headaches got worse, and eventually Roy had to tell the trainer about them. An MRI confirmed that his tumor had grown back, and a week later Roy had surgery to remove it.

Roy hated missing the end of his freshman season. By the time he left the hospital that winter, he had lost a lot of weight and muscle mass, but he was determined to win back his position that summer at training camp. He understood that the coach wasn't holding a slot for him. At this level of the game, college ball is essentially like the pros. It's fiercely competitive, and nobody gives you anything. If you want to start on a Division 1A team, you have fight for it.

So he began working out by himself in the spring: weight training, wind sprints, aerobic workouts. By summer he was back in shape and ready to compete. He won back his spot as a starter, and at the end of his second season he won the school's Most Courageous Athlete Award. Roy doesn't think of himself as being particularly courageous. But he's found out what he's made of.

"Football helped make me tough and disciplined," he explains. "Having to come back from brain surgery just made me tougher. When you've shared a ward with kids half your age who probably aren't going to make it till Christmas, and you see they're not complaining, it's pretty easy to get past the 'Why me?' questions. And it's pretty hard to get in a panic about anything that happens on a football field. If this brain tumor didn't break me, no offensive lineman is going to ruin my day."

His mother sent me a picture of Roy in his football uniform. He's a pretty fearsome looking guy: six-three, 275 pounds. Barbed-wire tattoos circle huge arms that can bench-press over 400 pounds. But behind his you-won't-get-past-me grimace, I can still see the smile of the second grader who just found out he gets to go skiing this winter.

FINDING THE COURAGE TO DO WHAT'S HARDEST DOESN'T usually mean rushing into a burning building to save someone. In real life, what's often scariest is the unknown.

Jackie Ross was one of those twelve-year-old girls who spends all day waiting to get back to the stable so she can ride her horse. Then, one day, she started to lose her balance and fall. I diagnosed and removed a benign tumor from her brain. Five months later she was back in the saddle. She wanted nothing more than to put the whole nightmare of her tumor behind her. But even though she made a splendid recovery, she discovered she wasn't quite the same person.

Every summer, the stable where she rode held a benefit horse show. Children with cerebral palsy and Down's syndrome were invited to ride with the healthy kids, who led them around the ring and coached them. Jackie had always participated out of a sense of obligation, but she never enjoyed herself. "I'm ashamed to say that I used to be a little afraid of the kids," Jackie admits. "I wanted to be nice to them, but I never really looked at them or talked to them."

That summer after her operation was different. Suddenly she had more in common with these kids than just a love of horses. She knew what it was like to be seen as different, to have people pity you and look past you when they talked. For five months Jackie had constantly felt self-conscious, as if the whole world were staring at her. She was the girl who had the brain tumor and wore weird glasses for her double vision. She was the one with a tremor in her right hand that made her handwriting shaky. She always took care to part her hair in a way that would cover the scar in the back of her head.

One girl in particular caught Jackie's attention the morning of the horse show. Alexis was Jackie's age and she had cerebral palsy. Jackie could tell that she loved to ride and wasn't afraid of looking strange or of falling off. She sat tall in the saddle, and she was proud and beautiful, even though she wore thick glasses. "When I called out adjustments to her, she was all business, and if she needed me to guide her or support her, she just reached out her arm. She really showed me her strength by acknowledging her limits—without any fear or shame.

"Seeing how determined Alexis was to ride a horse, when most people in her condition would never risk getting up out a wheelchair, really changed me," Jackie says. "After that morning, I never let myself feel ashamed again, and I never lost sight of what I wanted to accomplish."

For the next nine years, she stayed focused on becoming a better rider. There were some bumps in the road. She broke her collarbone, sprained a knee, and even ruptured her spleen, but nothing kept her from excelling at what she loved to do.

Last year, her college riding team won the NCAA National Equestrian Championship.

Jackie's favorite competitive event is jumping. "The thing about jumping," she explains, "is that it's scary, but you have to rein in your fear or you can't compete. A horse is hypersensitive, and if he picks up on your fear he'll tense up and he won't go over the jump. Your job is to keep him calm and relaxed, but psych him up for the jump at the same time. And while you're coaxing him toward the jump you're also psyching yourself up. If you hit the takeoff just right, he knows what to do—and suddenly this 2,000-pound animal under you is lifting you way off the ground, and you're flying. There's no other word to describe it. It's magical."

Even though she's been able to compete on a national level, Jackie still has a tremor in her right hand that she can't control. Like so many of my patients, she's way beyond seeing her imperfections as obstacles. "I spent a lot of time hoping my tremor would go away, but now I don't really care," she says. "It reminds me of all the things that used to scare me that don't anymore. It reminds me of all the fences I've jumped in the past ten years."

4

Believe in Miracles

Nothing is too wonderful to be true.

—Michael Faraday, 19th-century physicist

Some people say that there are no accidents. By which I guess they mean that we choose our lot in life, or that the twists and turns of our existence are chosen for us by God or by some grand design.

I don't buy that. I never have. Maybe it's the line of work I'm in.

It's hard to explain what it's like in a pediatric neurosurgical ward. The usual macho metaphors for life-and-death environments—a minefield, a tightrope, a bull-fighting ring—don't capture it. In many ways, going to work here is most like going to church or temple. It's where all of us—patients and their parents, doctors, nurses, chaplains, and social workers—face our deepest fears. Fear of failure, fear of death, fear of loss, fear of whatever it is that makes tumors grow in children's brains.

It's a journey of faith, inescapably a spiritual undertaking. You can't encounter something as inexplicable and unforgivable as tumors in young bodies without inquiring into areas that go beyond your rational understanding, beyond your surgical expertise. The responses to the twin questions we face every day—Why do children get sick? and How do we help them get better?—are only partly medical, and inevitably lead to other questions:

What is the role of hope in healing, and what do we do when there is no hope left?

How do we make sense of the terrible and wonderful things that happen for which there is no medical explanation? And if we can't explain these events, can we still believe in them?

How do we remain emotionally and spiritually open in the face of something so scary that it challenges our most basic assumptions about a just God and an orderly universe?

I don't know why kids get seriously sick, but I don't believe that calamities are visited on us to test our faith. What I do believe is that God endows each of us with special gifts, however unevenly and unfairly they may be distributed. How we use them to deal with adversity is up to us. I've often said to parents of patients, when confronted by a tough decision about whether or not to operate, "I wish God would tell us what to do. But for better or worse, we've got to make this call on our own."

You might think that after spending thirty years treating

kids with life-threatening brain tumors, it would be hard to believe in any kind of deity. The opposite is true. It's witnessing kids' grace under extraordinary pressure that renews my faith every day.

MIKEY SCHWARTZ WAS JUST TWO AND A HALF YEARS OLD when he was diagnosed with a malignant and fast-growing tumor in his cerebellum. Fortunately, it was still localized. When I removed his tumor, I was hopeful that we'd seen the last of it.

Radiation is not an option for young children because it retards brain growth, so over the next two years Mikey received an extended course of chemotherapy. During his treatment Mikey became one of the most adored children on the unit. Everyone loved him. It's hard to say why—he's simply a sweet, sweet soul. During Mikey's treatment, I also became friendly with his parents, Sam and Mindy. They lived in Manhattan and, like my family, they spent the December holiday in Florida.

The week before Christmas, two years after his surgery, Mikey was back at the hospital for his every-six-month MRI. His mother was up in the children's playroom wrapping holiday gifts. I was already on vacation with my family in Florida, where we had planned to meet up with Mikey and his parents the following week to share a holiday meal.

I was in the middle of a tennis game when my cell phone rang. It was Tania Maher, my triage nurse at the INN. "Fred, you have to get back up here. Mikey's had a recurrence." I flew up that afternoon and went straight to the hospital. It was almost midnight when I found Sam and Mindy standing over Mikey's bed, watching him sleep. I hugged them and urged them not to lose hope. I assured them that we still had lots of treatment options left.

"When I saw Mikey's MRIs this afternoon," said Sam, "I was so filled with rage that I cursed out loud. I kept shouting, 'God damn it! God damn it!' The question I keep asking myself is, Why would God let this happen again? How could He put Mikey and us through this misery all over again?"

The Schwartzes weren't a religious or observant family, but over the years I've found that there are no atheists in the OR. It doesn't matter whether you're secular or religious, Jewish or Christian, Hindu or Moslem. When your child gets seriously sick, you find yourself plunged into a passionate dialogue with God. Anger is as good an icebreaker as any.

I've also found that when you're filled with anger and fear, it helps to be able to believe. It doesn't matter what you believe in—I've seen kids sustained through terrible ordeals by their belief in Tinkerbell—as long as you believe in *something*. Even if it's just a God to curse and berate. If you don't believe in anything, you're sunk.

I know from working with families of every religious background that those with some kind of spiritual framework for their crisis do much better. Not that faith comes easily in the face of a child's life-threatening illness. But it definitely helps to have a larger spiritual context for a child's suffering, and the pain it makes a family endure. The parents with more flexible theologies seem to do better than those with more rigid models. If they can't conceive of a just world where bad things *do* happen to good people, their anger at God can blot out every other emotion.

I was awash in my own mix of emotions the next morning as I paced in my office, preparing to operate on Mikey. His latest MRI was clipped to the light box in my office, and I was trying to visualize what his tumor would look like under the operating microscope. I wondered if I'd be able to get it all this time. Rabbi Mychal Springer, our chaplain at the time, poked her head inside the door. "Fred, how would you feel about praying with Sam and Mindy before you go into the OR?"

If you know Mychal, you'd understand that this was strictly a rhetorical question. In my experience, clergy are like every other group of professionals; some are competent, some are expert, and some are a pain in the ass. Mychal is in a category by herself: highly gifted, and immensely soulful. She looks like a petite teenager, though she's actually in her mid-thirties, and you wouldn't think so much soul could fit inside such a small person. She's a dynamo. Some people can be described as a force of nature; Mychal is a force of God.

As our chaplain, she had one of the toughest jobs at the INN—to offer people hope when hope feels out of reach, to help show them the way back to what they believe in when they're lost in grief or panic. Mychal has an uncanny instinct for speaking to children and adults in their own spiritual idiom, whatever their faith. Praying with Mychal is always an adventure. She jumps right in and addresses God as if He were standing there beside you, or perhaps just behind the drawn curtain in the ICU. Her prayers are never scripted, always spontaneous expressions of hope and humility. Since coming on board as our founding chaplain, Mychal had become *my* rabbi too.

So when she appeared in my office to invite me to pray with Mikey's parents, I didn't think twice about it. I'd never actually prayed right before surgery—certainly not with the family of the patient. But standing there in front of the light box, staring glumly at pictures of a tumor that had already resisted surgery and chemo, I welcomed her offer.

Dressed in my scrubs and operating clogs, I followed Mychal down the hall to the intensive care unit. Mikey was already in the OR being prepped for surgery. Sam and Mindy were standing beside an empty bed in the ICU where we'd be bringing Mikey in a few hours. They looked like they hadn't slept much the night before. Mychal pulled the curtain closed around us, shutting out the monitors and IV poles for a moment. The four of us held hands around the empty bed. Holding hands helps, whether you're six or sixty. I've always found that making physical contact with patients and their families is the best way to dispel the loneliness that infects the fear we're all feeling. I'm a toucher. I feel better when I'm touching someone, so I figure they must feel better too.

So we held hands while Mychal led us in prayer. That morning Mychal prayed in Hebrew and in English for Mikey's recovery. She asked God to watch over the bed we stood around, and she asked Him to watch over the operating table downstairs. Finally, she prayed, "And please, God, guide Fred's hands so he can once and for all get rid of that stupid tumor in Mikey's head."

Sam is ordinarily a buttoned-up guy, a hard-nosed corporate attorney in his day job. But being the father of a sick son wasn't his day job. "If I was ever going to pray," Sam says now, "this was the time. As I prayed I could feel the warm tears running down my face. They weren't tears of sadness or despair. They were tears of hope. As strange as it sounds, all my anger from the day before dissolved into gratitude. I was grateful that we had some treatment options left to feel hopeful about. I was grateful that we could hold each other's hands and pray together."

Mychal thinks of prayer simply as opening your heart and giving it a voice. "Whenever you open your heart," she says, "things can happen that are beyond our understanding." What happened that morning was that by holding hands and opening our hearts, we were able to transform a moment of anger and fear into a moment of hope.

Keeping our hearts open in the midst of despair is what prayer's all about. Children evoke our greatest love and our greatest fear. When our feelings become overwhelming, we tend to shut them off. Mychal will tell you that all emotions can heal us—because they all open our hearts. All emotions, including anger, are sacred. "Anger is part of every relationship, including with God," says Mychal. "But people are afraid of getting angry and alienating God when they need God most. 'I'm angry *and* I love you' is the toughest statement for most people, whoever they're speaking to."

After we finished praying, Sam invited Mychal to Mikey's bar mitzvah, which was still nine years off. Then I went downstairs to the OR and took out Mikey's "stupid" tumor—and prayed to God that it wouldn't come back.

I can't say if my hands were guided that day. But I do know that I felt Mikey's parents beside me in the OR, and I felt the force of their love for their son. Praying with them made the OR a sacred space for me that morning. And as their son's surgeon, that made me feel more powerful.

Today, six years later, Mikey's a rambunctious ten-year-old boy. He went to sleep-away camp for the first time this summer. Last month he was back at the hospital for an MRI—his eighth clean scan in a row—and afterward he played a raucous game of stickball in the hallway with Jeff Allen, our senior neuro-oncologist.

I don't believe God cured Mikey of his cancer—any more

than I believe God made him sick in the first place. I believe Mikey's alive today because he's got a loving family and a committed and talented medical team who refused to give up on him, who pooled their God-given talents to defeat one stupid tumor and save one sweet soul from a disease that most doctors will tell you is incurable.

HOPE AND FAITH PLAY A HUGE PART IN EVERY PATIENT'S recovery—and in the survival of every patient's family. A parent of one of my patients asked their previous surgeon if there was any hope for her son, to which the surgeon replied, "It's not my job to offer hope." I emphatically argue the inverse: It's not a doctor's job to deprive a patient or a family of hope. None of us is God; none of us knows who will live and who will die.

Every tumor is different, and every child is unique. I've never felt I could say "I'm sure" about any patient's prognosis. I've seen kids die who should have been cured. And I've had other patients who, by all the laws of medicine, should have died a decade ago who are playing professional sports today. Some people call them miracles. Others see them as statistical anomalies. From my point of view, the odds of a child's survival are meaningless in any particular case. What often makes the difference for patients and their families is how long they can cling to a lifeline of hope during a storm that often seems interminable.

At the age of twelve, Danny Trush's life revolved around basketball. His greatest joy was shooting hoops; his most revered heroes were the New York Knicks. Every Sunday during the winter and spring he played in a league game, and his family was always there to root for him. In the fourth quarter of a game one March, Danny dribbled down the court and lofted the ball toward the basket. Suddenly he clutched his head in pain, staggered to the sideline, and collapsed into his father's arms.

By the time he arrived across town at the INN, Danny was already in a coma. An MRI revealed five aneurisms in his brain that had probably been there since birth. One of these vascular malformations had burst, hemorrhaging blood into the space between his brain and his skull.

This kid was in desperate shape. It took everyone's skill just to keep him alive—surgeons, intensivists in the ICU, nurses, and a team of neuroradiologists. His bleed created pressure on his cranium that was cutting off the flow of oxygen to his brain. We couldn't control the pressure by any of the usual means—in fact, the pressure readings in his brain were the highest we'd ever recorded. We drained blood and fluid from his skull, but that didn't work. Neither did medication. In the days that followed, the pressure building in his cranium triggered several strokes that would normally have been fatal. Meanwhile, tests we ran to measure electrical and brain wave activity showed almost none. While I never give up hope for a patient, I felt I had to prepare Danny's parents to say farewell to their oldest son.

His family was reeling under the worst kind of strain. But they never collapsed. As the days stretched into weeks, they learned to pace themselves and work together to make sure that Danny had loved ones by his side around the clock. His father, Ken, stayed with him every night. In the morning, his mother, Nancy, relieved Ken so he could go to work. She stayed with Danny all day, every day, and his younger brother, Michael, joined them every afternoon. Ken wrote daily e-mails to their family and friends to keep them updated on Danny's condition. Since he remained in a coma, there wasn't really much to report except, "He's still alive." And there wasn't much hope left to cling to. As Ken remembers, "When there was nothing left to do medically, we had to fall back on our instincts, which were love, prayer, and faith." They clung to their belief in a higher power, and to their trust in the recuperative power of the 90 percent of the human brain that we don't understand.

When Danny's coma entered its third week, I tried to keep up his family's spirits. "Children are special," I told them. "You never know." But I'd never seen anyone revive from his level of brain damage. With no conventional medical options remaining, we decided to try an experiment. Maybe if we drained some fluid from his spine, it would reduce the pressure at the base of his skull. The day after the procedure, Danny's cranial pressure stabilized. A few days later, on Easter

Sunday, Danny poked his father with his toe. Ken wasn't sure whether or not it was simply a reflex. "Did you just kick me in the butt?" he asked his son. Danny smiled faintly. Since a sense of humor arises from a high-functioning part of the brain, we all drew some hope from that little smile.

Seven days passed without any other signs of consciousness. Then, one morning, almost a month after going into a coma, Danny opened his eyes. His unlikely journey back to life had begun, but he still had miles of recovery in front of him. His weight was down to sixty-five pounds. He couldn't talk, but he could blink yes-no responses.

We clipped his remaining four aneurisms to keep them from hemorrhaging. A few weeks later we transferred Danny downtown to the Rusk Institute to begin his rehabilitation. Howard Rusk, the legendary founder of that medical center, once likened a successful rehab process to the transformation that occurs inside a fiery kiln; gravely injured patients enter as rough clay and emerge as fine china. That's a pretty good metaphor for Danny's recovery—except he turned out to be a lot less fragile than china.

When he first got to Rusk, Danny couldn't move at all. He had to be lifted into a wheelchair. It was weeks before he could hold a pencil and months before he could stand erect. One night, Ken and a nurse were giving Danny a shower when he began to speak again for the first time. His voice had dropped an octave during his coma; Danny would never speak with a boy's voice again.

From the beginning of his rehab, Danny displayed the determination of an Olympic athlete. He never lost his sense of humor. And he never lost his sense of purpose—to claw back every precious piece of his life that he could reclaim. After 341 days in the hospital and in rehab, Danny wheeled himself out of the Rusk Institute and into the rest of his life.

So many people, including medical professionals, want to sets limits on the brain's potential for self-healing and recovery. I think it's because boundaries, no matter how arbitrary, help make the seat of human consciousness seem less mysterious, more measurable. Danny sent us all a loud and clear message: "Don't set limits." He's certainly defied the limits of what I imagined he'd be capable of. Even though I believed it might be possible for him to reclaim a quality life, I couldn't actually imagine it.

Now I don't have to. I only have to watch Danny continue to progress month by month, year by year. Today, five years after his hemorrhage, he keeps rewriting the record book. A couple of years ago, I asked his physical therapist to predict the outer limit of Danny's remarkable recovery. "How far will Danny go?" she pondered with a smile. "I imagine, as far as he wants to."

Danny's not "perfect." He's human. He's still got some short-term memory and processing problems, but not enough to discourage him. His parents have made sure he's had all the educational support he needs. At eighteen, he's getting A's in his senior year of high school and is heading to college. He still has weakness in his left arm and right leg, but nothing he's not determined to overcome. As his father says, "We love him as he is today, and have hope for tomorrow. With love and support, there's nothing Danny can't accomplish." Danny's one of the most self-assured people you'll meet. Ask him about his goals, and he'll tell you, "I just try my hardest every day and I know I won't be disappointed."

Recently, Danny decided he wanted to become an athlete again. "I wanted to run," he says matter-of-factly. "It's something I always felt I would do again, even when I could barely walk." He works out twice a week now with the Achilles Track Club, which helps disabled people train for mainstream competitive races. The name fits for the kind of hero Danny's become to everyone who crosses his path. Right now he's training to run New York City's Fifth Avenue Mile race.

A few months ago I got a visit from Danny in my hospital room. It was an emotional encounter—doctor and patient, both unlikely survivors of monthlong comas, fellow travelers in the marathon of rehab. We embraced each other with our strongest two arms—his right, my left.

Danny told me about his training regimen for the Fifth Avenue Mile. He's completed it before, but never at a run. The year after he emerged from his coma, when he was still in a wheelchair, he walked the mile in forty-five minutes with two people holding him up. The next year it took him eighteen minutes with a person supporting him on either side. The next year, fifteen minutes, with just one person to hold on to.

"This year," he told me, "I'm going to run it—on my own."

WE'VE BECOME SO SUPERRATIONAL—PARTICULARLY THE medical professionals who try to reduce the healing arts to a precise science—that we've distanced ourselves from the miraculous. Yet miracles are irrefutably a part of our lives. I don't think of miracles as supernatural events. To me they're the contact point between the human and the divine. Miracles are what happen when the things we most hope for—the things that seem impossible—become possible. That's the miracle of everyday life: the miracle of hope.

Medical people often feel threatened by the hope for miracles; to them it means the patient or his family is in denial, or else that they have unfair expectations of their doctors. Donna Fields, the mother of one of my patients, was told by her son's first doctor, "Take him home and let him die in peace." But her family's reserves of hope weren't exhausted yet. They hung a sign over their son's bed that read, WE EXPECT A MIRACLE. As different doctors and nurses encountered the sign on rounds they would ask her, "Mrs. Fields, do you understand your son's diagnosis?"

"Indeed we did!" says Donna six years later, as she watches her son play tetherball in her backyard. "We knew we had to reach deep, deep inside our spirit and truly trust God to take us through this. Afterwards, when we found our way to the INN, we got our hope back. And our son's future."

Children have a prodigious aptitude for faith in miraculously happy endings. One of my patients, a nine-year-old boy named Mark, had to go through a year of chemotherapy before he finally beat his tumor. He was a real fighter. Our chaplain, Mychal, was curious to know what got him through his toughest times, so she asked him if he ever prayed. Yes, Mark replied, he prayed by reciting the blessing over the Hanukkah candles.

At first, Mychal found his answer dispiriting. As a rabbi, she viewed Hanukkah as a minor Jewish holiday that had been elevated in recent decades to compete with Christmas. "Is this all we teach our children about prayer, about speaking to God?" she thought to herself. "A boy is fighting for his life and the only prayer he has to fall back on is the blessing over the Hanukkah candles."

Then she recalled the words of the second blessing over the candles: *Baruch atah Adonai eloheinu melech ha-olam, she-asa nisim l'avoteinu, ba-yamim ha-hem, ba-z'man ha-zeh.* "Praised be Thou O Lord our God, who worked miracles for our ancestors in days long ago at this season." It was only then that she realized that by invoking the spirit of Hanukkah, Mark had called on God's miracle-making powers at a time when he desperately needed one.

Hanukkah is the story of the victory of the few over the

many, the triumph of hope over despair. Two thousand years ago, Judah Maccabee's small army of Israelites miraculously overcame the massive Assyrian army. They reclaimed the Temple in Jerusalem to find that there was only enough oil to keep the sacred Temple lamp lit for a day. In a second miracle, the lamp remained aflame for eight days and nights, until a fresh supply of oil arrived.

The lesson of Hanukkah is that when all hope seems exhausted, our faith can sustain us. Miracles happen. Hanukkah, as well as Christmas, calls on us to live with an openness to the possibility of miracles. When our souls are in danger of shutting down in the face of life's bitterness, these redemptive stories remind us that all is not foretold.

Another patient of mine, a nine-year-old boy named Anthony, had a particularly aggressive brain tumor and a terrible prognosis. The medical staff and the family thought we had come to the end of the line, though we still prayed for a good outcome. Anthony was raised in a religious Christian family and was active in his church. He couldn't conceive of anything bad happening in his life. Even though he realized that his medical condition was dire, he clung to his hope for the future. He loved the New Testament, and he found particular strength in the story of Jesus on the cross bearing all that pain, but for a reason. Because he was God's chosen one, Jesus's suffering wasn't meaningless. And because Anthony believed that—despite his brain tumor—he was one of God's chosen, he had faith that he would recover.

Anthony is alive and well today, seven years later. I can't say why he survived. Was he simply lucky? Were his and our prayers answered? Was his faith simply stronger than his disease? I doubt Anthony would be alive today if his faith hadn't been so alive in his heart.

One of Mychal's aphorisms is never far from my mind: *Faith is a journey.* When we're lost in a dark wood and we need to find our way home, prayer is as good a path as we're likely to find. When Mychal came to the INN as its founding chaplain, I told her I wanted her to run a weekly prayer circle, one where everybody—patients, their families, doctors, nurses, nonmedical staff—could replenish their hope regardless of their religious background. She held these prayer meetings every Friday morning in the children's playroom. I came to them; the other surgeons came. So did the nurses and rehab therapists. Even the people on the cleaning crews came. We all needed to renew ourselves, and praying alongside our patients and their families reminded each of us that we were all in this together.

Mychal would start with an opening prayer for the children and ask for wisdom and healing for the staff and the parents. Then people would offer up their own prayers. There was music and singing. We would always sing a round of "This Little Light of Mine," inserting each child's name in the refrain: "This little light of Kevin, I'm going to let it shine . . ." We'd go around the whole room and bless every child.

I remember one Friday morning a boy named Gary was sitting at the computer in the playroom with his back to the prayer group. All I could see was an angry scar that ran down the back of his skull. I'd seen him there the Friday before. On this morning, Mychal included him in the song: "This little light of Gary, I'm going to let it shine, let it shine, let it shine, let it shine." Gary turned around and he was smiling as if a sun had risen inside him. He turned back to his computer, but the next Friday morning Gary was standing in the circle with the rest of us.

An Orthodox Jewish man, whose son was a patient of mine, also found a place in our circle. He was very religious, but for a long time he wasn't comfortable coming to the prayer meetings. They were multifaith, they were conducted by a woman, and they were foreign to the way he was used to praying. His son continued to struggle medically, and the father continued to suffer. As the weeks went by, he began to hover around the edges of our prayer meetings. Then one Friday morning he brought his son with him. Mychal welcomed them by leading the group in singing *"Shalom Aleichem"*—"Peace Unto You"—the greeting of the Sabbath angel that Jews sing at Sabbath dinner on Friday night. Most of the people around the playroom that morning couldn't speak Hebrew, but they all sang *"Shalom Aleichem"* in greeting to this father and son for whom our prayer circle had finally become home.

WHAT DO YOU DO WHEN THERE IS NO HOPE LEFT? THIS is the toughest question of all. The doctors don't want to give up and admit defeat, and parents can't bear to let go of the child they love more than their own life. Surrendering a child to death goes against every parent's and doctor's instinct. It goes against nature.

I fight like hell for every child in my care, but sometimes it's my job to lay down my arms and make peace with the inevitable. Letting go is even harder for parents. The most heartbreaking situation is when a child is ready to die, but her parents can't bring themselves to release her. On occasion, I've seen a child help her parents say good-bye.

Emily was a thirteen-year-old in the terminal phase of brain cancer. She'd had a three-year remission after surgery, but when her tumor grew back, a second round of chemo did nothing to slow it down. She began to lose her balance. Her vision began to blur. Her parents were frantic, of course. They wanted me to operate again, but it would only have caused Emily more suffering at that point.

As is often the case with terminally ill children, Emily knew she was going to die before many of the adults were willing to admit it. Emily was a spirited fighter—she knew her mind, and could be as combative as she was playful—but she was worn out by her three-year battle. She still drew in the children's playroom each morning, but she couldn't sit up for more than half an hour without having to lie down and rest.

When she asked the staff about her condition, we were honest with her. But she couldn't talk to her parents about it. When she'd try, they'd cut her off and insist that she stop being negative. Fortunately, her older sister, Rachel, didn't shut her down when she wanted to talk about death. Rachel was an unusually mature fifteen-year-old who had grown up in a hurry during Emily's three-year illness. And like many siblings of sick kids, she learned to step into a parental role when her parents were lost in grief.

Near the end, while the family was keeping a nonstop vigil by her bedside, Emily decided to address her parents directly. She waited until Rachel arrived after school, took her hand, and turned to her mother and father. "I need to go now. I know how much you love me. I've got to go, but you know that part of me will always be here with you."

Emily's parents looked at each other and cried. They hugged Rachel, and held on to both of Emily's hands, still afraid to let go. Then Rachel pushed the parents' sleeping-in bed next to Emily's and the four of them lay down together. Emily died later that night.

SOMETIMES A CHILD CAN BE A BEACON OF HOPE TO HER parents, even when disease is eating away at hope. Jenna Kamil has become part of the INN's lore, not so much because of the storybook elements of her life and death, but because of the way her spirit continues to infuse the rooms and corridors of the hospital. Her story tells us about the limits of medicine and the limitless dimension of the human heart.

Jenna was diagnosed with a malignant brain stem tumor at the age of five. From the start it was a bad-dream case. I was only able to resect part of her tumor, and she suffered nerve damage during surgery that interfered with her speech, breathing, and swallowing. I honestly couldn't hold out any hope to her parents, Gideon and Linda.

Over the next six weeks, Jenna confounded all our expectations. Even with limited speech, she managed to bond with everyone on the floor. She was gentle and tough in equal measure, and she never lost her smile. Every day she'd go to the playroom and pursue her art projects with a fierce determination. The recurrent themes in her art were colorful flowers and rainbows. Through her drawings and her joyous manner, Jenna managed to bring light and beauty into an often dark and scary place.

She was the kind of patient the staff loved to pamper. One day, the nurses treated her to a spa day, complete with shampoo and styling, nails and massage. The day she left the hospital for home, Jenna told the orderly to halt her wheelchair as she was exiting past the head nurse's station. Jenna reminded the nurse that she had promised to give her a French braid, and Jenna refused to leave without it. Combs, bobby pins, and a mirror were hastily assembled, and Jenna got her braid.

Once she got home, Jenna made what I can only call a miraculous recovery. Little by little she regained the functions she had lost. Then she returned to the life she loved: ballet, karate, kindergarten, playtime with her friends and younger brother, vacations with her family. She never missed a day of school. Even on bad days, when it took her hours to get ready and she had to be carried into class, Jenna was determined to be with her classmates. And they were equally determined to have her there.

Her remission only lasted about ten months, but the Kamils made the most of it. Buoyed by Jenna's irrepressible enthusiasm, they savored every moment and managed to forestall their dread of the future.

When Jenna's symptoms returned, we operated again. But it didn't help. Jenna was confined to the INN as her health deteriorated. When the nurses asked her if she had a wish, Jenna responded, "I wish the world would stay a rainbow." She kept on drawing, and kept on living. She wrote and illustrated a mini-autobiography, that read in part:

> *My name is Jenna. I am six years old.*
> *This is a story about when I became ill.*
> *I was five years old. I felt sad and scared.*

> *Here are some ways my life has changed . . .*
> *I can't talk right now. I have machines in my room.*
> *This makes me feel a little sad.*
> *I go to the hospital to have radiation treatments. At first I felt scared.*
> *But now it's OK.*

I can't eat or drink. I miss eating everything.
This makes me feel very sad.

Here are some ways my life has stayed the same. . . .
I still do arts and crafts.
I still play with Jesse, my brother, and my friends.
I dance in my ballet class. .
I do karate. I am a yellow belt now.
We are still a family.

A week later, Jenna went home with her family to die in her own bed. We went to her funeral, and afterward we went back to her house to sit with the family. As we approached the house, we noticed that everyone was standing beside their cars, looking up at the sky and pointing. There, arched over the Kamils' house, was a bold and beautiful rainbow, unbroken from end to end. The same rainbow returned each afternoon for three days, as if in echo of Jenna's joyful and comforting smile.

Jenna's sign—it was hard to experience it any other way—had special meaning for her parents. Gideon and Linda were not religious people, but when Jenna died, the medical part of their ordeal ended and a spiritual journey began. For years they had lived in terror of losing their child. What they discovered is that Jenna's soul is something eternal that no disease could kill, that death could never vanquish. She remains a constant presence in their lives, and in the life of the INN.

Gideon and Linda remembered Jenna's wish that the world remain a rainbow. They started a foundation, Jenna's Rainbow, to try to make the world a rainbow for children and families who were traveling their own dark and lonely road in the fight against cancer. They do whatever they can to fill needs as they arise—home care, hot meals, plane tickets—whatever will comfort a child or family in need. It's their way of celebrating Jenna's life. And by keeping her spirit alive at the INN, they remind all of us to take a moment each day to look up to the sky and search for rainbows.

IT'S BEEN SAID, "TO HAVE CHILDREN IS TO GIVE HOSTAGES to fortune." All parents live in dread of their child becoming seriously ill, and they pray that it will never happen. When it does, their hearts are ransomed to fear. They have to walk a treacherous tightrope between despair and hope, between terror and courage.

I meet these parents when they come to my office, clutching MRI films in one hand and their sick child in the other. They come from across the country and around the world. During a single week last year, I operated on a Hindu girl from India, a Greek Orthodox boy from Athens, and a seventeen-year-old Buddhist monk in training from Tibet. Their parents' responses to their personal crises were as diverse as their backgrounds. And yet, having a sick child tends to erase all cultural difference. Every parent has to face his or her apocalypse from scratch, has to cope with the fear and the anger, has to fight for faith with whatever tools they have.

My own test of faith began with a phone call I got at my office four years ago. It was the Friday of Columbus Day weekend, a busy morning at the INN, like most mornings. I was due in the operating room in a few minutes, and a doctor was coming in from out of town that day to interview for a position on our staff.

At the moment, I was on the phone with Jim, the boyfriend of my younger daughter, Ilana. It was like a scene out of a '40s movie. He had called to ask my permission to marry Ilana—but he was having trouble getting to the punch line. For the past five minutes he had been telling me how much Ilana meant to him, how much he loved her, and would always love her. I remember thinking how quaint the whole ritual was, how old-world. It was one of the things I liked best about Jim.

My assistant, Donna, came on the intercom. "It's Samara on line three. From Boston." Samara, my older daughter, was a second-year student at Harvard Business School. Though I spent altogether too much time at the hospital while my kids were growing up, I always stopped what I was doing to take their phone calls. I cut into Jim's monologue, "Jim, if she'll have you, marry her. I'm sure you'll both be very happy. Welcome to the family."

Then I got on the line with Samara. She was trying to keep her voice steady, but she was on the verge of tears. "Daddy, the doctor here found a lump in my neck. In my lymph node."

That was the moment the world stopped for me. The moment when my life as a pediatric neurosurgeon collided head-on with my life as a parent. Everything ground to a sickening, screeching halt.

Samara is a passionate runner, and a week earlier she had called complaining of allergy attacks that left her short of breath. I had prescribed some allergy medication, but when it didn't seem to be working, I had urged her to go the university health services to get it checked out. The doctor who examined her discovered a mass in the lymph nodes in her neck.

"They want me to have a CT scan," she told me now, her voice beginning to break, "but it's a holiday weekend, so they can't do it until Tuesday."

"Samara, get on a plane today. This afternoon." I struggled to keep my own voice calm, but I could feel the blood racing through my head. "Come home and we'll take care of you."

Donna's voice came on the intercom again. "Fred, they're waiting for you in the OR. Are you ready?"

I had our chief radiologist do Samara's CT scan later that afternoon, but we wouldn't have the biopsy results from her lymph node until Monday. That turned into the longest weekend of my life. As it happened, Ilana and Jim were spending the weekend on Fire Island, where we knew Jim planned to propose. Rather than spoil it for them before we had any hard information, we all decided to hold off telling them anything.

Samara slept in her old room, along with our dog. I barely slept at all. I was left alone with my fears, pacing the house until close to dawn, looking in on Samara every hour or so. I remembered sitting in that same bed with Samara as a child, reading *Sleeping Beauty* aloud to her. Now I was the powerless king who couldn't protect his daughter from the witch's deadly curse, no matter how many spinning wheels he burned or banished.

In spite of my macho surgeon credentials, I had always been a wimp when it came to my own children's accidents and illnesses. Ilana's migraines and Joey's asthma attacks sent me into a panic. Kathy had always been the rock on the home front.

The biopsy results on Monday confirmed my suspicion: Samara had Hodgkin's disease, cancer of the lymph nodes. As a doctor, I knew that we had caught Samara's cancer at an early stage and that with prompt treatment she had a good chance of a full recovery. But for a parent, anytime the odds of a cure for your child are less than 100 percent, they stink. After I got off the phone with the pathologist, I remember thinking, "This is the test of courage I never wanted to have to pass."

Samara insisted that she wanted to go back to school and be treated in Boston, so I went into crisis-management mode.

I spent the evening on the phone with colleagues at Massachusetts General in Boston, assembling a team of specialists to take care of my daughter. At ten o'clock that night, Ilana returned from Fire Island with an engagement ring and a cat-who-ate-the-canary grin on her face. After we shared the hard news and tears with Ilana, Samara said with her trademark dry humor, "This is great. You get a diamond and I get cancer."

Later that week, Kathy and I flew back to Boston with Samara and met with the oncologist at Mass General. He explained the treatment—five months of chemotherapy, followed by radiation—and the side effects Samara could expect, the same ones I myself had recited to countless parents. When we left the oncologist's office, Samara and Kathy sat down on a bench in the hallway and wept. I'll never forget the sight of them sitting there, holding each other and crying. I never felt so powerless and so afraid.

Kathy and I flew up to Boston every other Friday for Samara's chemo. I flew back on Saturday morning to be with our boys at home while Kathy stayed behind to care for Samara. I went to work and pulled myself together so I could take care of my patients. I fought against the paralysis of depression. I got a lot of support from my extended family at the INN—our staff, patients, and their parents. They brought me food, wrote me letters, gave me hugs. It didn't make the pain go away, but it helped keep hope alive—and without hope there is only fear.

There wasn't anything edifying or ennobling about the

pain of watching Samara suffer through her treatment. Every young woman's first anxiety about chemo seems to be, "Will I lose my hair?" I've heard it from hundreds of patients. But when Samara asked me the same question, I went to pieces. I didn't want to go into the room the first day Samara was getting chemo. I didn't want to watch anyone stick a needle into her. I went and I watched, and I'm here to tell you that there wasn't any take-away wisdom from watching her body battle against a deadly disease and its toxic remedies—watching her lose weight and strength, watching her beautiful blond hair fall out in handfuls.

The same year that Samara endured twice-monthly chemo for five months, followed by daily radiation for six weeks, she graduated from Harvard Business School and landed a job at a leading financial firm in Manhattan. In the spring she helped Ilana plan her wedding, and in July she walked down the aisle as her maid of honor, her hair in a chic, ultrashort style. Samara's been in remission now for several years, and she has a good prognosis. Hopefully, she's cured.

Despite my horror at what she's been through, I recognize that Samara emerged from her ordeal a more self-confident and mature person. She's mentored other young women with Hodgkin's who have become close friends. She enjoys a renewed feeling of health and physical strength. She's taken up distance running and has competed in two marathons. And as with so many of my young patients, surviving her nightmare has fortified Samara's spirit. It's strengthened her belief in God, while giving her a greater appreciation for the fragility of His creation. For Samara, understanding that the world is an imperfect place—a place where terrible things sometimes happen to good people—has made God more accessible and alive.

Here's how she assesses her life today: "I like the person I am, and am still becoming. The experience of Hodgkin's disease is inseparable from that. I wouldn't wish it on anyone else, but I can't imagine myself any other way."

Regardless of everything I've learned about the resilience of young people, it's been hard for me to trust in Samara's special strengths. As much as I take heart from her vitality, the parent in me continues to suffer. Every time she goes in for her six-month checkup I wince where it still hurts inside, where my heart still hasn't healed.

When a child gets sick, a parent's job description changes radically overnight—and it's a job none of us is trained for, as I found out. I know now, in a way that I had only witnessed before, how desperately every parent of a sick child has to fight for his or her own survival and healing. For parents, as much as for doctors, the challenge is to remain open. Even if it's your child who's fighting for survival, there's a natural tendency to shut down your mind and parts of your emotions—the parts that are hardest to deal with.

Over the years, some of our medical staff who are parents

have confided to me the deal they make with God: "I'll devote myself to these sick children if you spare mine." Personally, I'd never been able to enter into that kind of negotiation. I don't believe that God causes children to become sick, or protects them from harm. I believe that He endows us with whatever strength we need to endure adversity. After that we're on our own.

But that didn't keep me from praying for Samara's life. I would have made any deal to save her. I was a father, and my little girl was sick.

Samara's illness brought me to my knees as nothing else has, before or since. When you're down at ground level, you realize that our humanity is measured by our power to love, to feel pain, and to persevere.

5

Play to Your Strengths

*I don't think I shall easily bow down before the blows
that inevitably come to everyone.*

—Anne Frank

Kids love scary stories, especially stories about young people in peril. Children of every generation are drawn to these tales of daring kids facing off against evil: Hansel and Gretel outwitting the wicked witch; the young David doing battle with the fearsome giant Goliath, armed only with a slingshot and his faith in God; Luke Skywalker invoking The Force in his combat-to-the-death with Darth Vader. These enduring stories are about resourceful youngsters who, when confronted by extreme adversity, discovered hidden strengths they never knew they possessed. Harry Potter comes to appreciate the true power of his parents' legacy. Dorothy discovers that the protective properties she attributed to her ruby slippers reside, in fact, in her heart. Whatever their source, these hidden strengths emerge in moments of crisis to deliver children from danger.

Adults love these stories too because they remind us of the link between our vulnerability and our resilience. They show us how the same qualities of youth that make us feel most exposed and alive—our openness to joy and pain, faith and hope—can become the sources of our greatest power.

The moral of these stories can be summed up in two words: save yourself. We may well draw our inner strength from a source outside ourselves—from our ancestors, from our family, or from our God. But when we're staring death and destruction in the face, we can't afford to wait for Prince Charming or a fairy godmother to rescue us. Seriously ill children understand this truth intuitively. If they're lucky, they have family, friends, and doctors to lend them a hand. But kids know that their own determination to survive and adapt is their best hope for survival.

When Max Rheinhold was eight years old, I removed a malignant tumor from the occipital parietal area of his brain. Max was fortunate that his is one of the few types of brain cancer we can often cure. But because of their location, removing these tumors usually causes severe vision loss. In Max's case, he was left with vision in only one quadrant of one eye.

Crossing the street in his native Manhattan became a perilous adventure. Max's lack of peripheral vision also became a serious learning disability, since it was hard for him to see much of what was going on in class. He also missed a lot of the visual social cues that the rest of us take for granted, such as hand gestures, facial expressions, and body language. But the biggest loss for Max was the camaraderie of his basketball team. Though he rejoined the team after his postoperative chemotherapy and radiation, he couldn't play competitively. He loved shooting hoops, but most of all he loved being a team player.

Max's brain tumor robbed him of most of his eyesight but none of his heart. "I realized that just because I had lost part of my vision, I hadn't lost part of myself," he says. Within a few years, he found a new team—the school chorus. He joined the school newspaper and soon became the sports editor. As his reporting and writing skills grew, so did his self-confidence. He became a regular contributor to the Children's Brain Tumor Foundation's newsletter and website. He got into an academically rigorous Quaker high school, Friends Seminary, worked hard to adapt his learning style to his vision deficit, and earned a National Merit Scholar Commendation. He won several scholarships and is now a freshman at NYU.

Max now refers to the ten years since his diagnosis and treatment as his "extra life"—a gift he credits with making him a stronger, more optimistic, and more compassionate person. "I now realize that you can express your passions through many different channels," says Max. "If not for my brain tumor, I probably would never have experienced the joy and fulfillment I've found through singing and writing."

Quakers have an expression that Max heard a lot at his

high school: "Let your life speak." It's only recently that Max came to appreciate the meaning of that phrase. "For me, 'Let your life speak' means that your life has a voice of its own. No matter what happens, no matter what gets taken away from you, the best that's inside you will express itself. As long as you remain true to yourself, your life will speak. Not through words, but through deeds."

AMONG MY YOUNG PATIENTS AND THEIR FAMILIES, resilience is the trait that consistently separates the survivors from those who are torn apart by adversity. I suspect this is the same outside a hospital ward. In business, in love, in any endeavor that challenges our reserves of strength and hope, it's the most resilient among us who survive and eventually thrive. Misfortune, heartbreak, illness, and injury are inescapable events in all our lives. How we respond to misfortune is the key determinant of our ability to thrive.

This isn't just anecdotal. Countless sociological and psychological studies confirm that resilience—rather than intelligence or talent or even luck—is the primary determinant of success or failure in life. Long-term studies have tracked the careers, marriages, and family lives of children who grew up in the midst of extreme poverty, or who suffered abuse, or who suffered from physical or psychological handicaps. These severe childhood disadvantages proved to be less accurate predictors of adult happiness and success than the individual's ability to adapt, adjust, and persevere.

Physically and emotionally, children are amazingly resilient. All parents witness this truth on a daily basis, as their children bounce back from illness or disappointment in a matter of days, sometime minutes. In a pediatric neurosurgery ward, it's even more dramatic. Children often get up and walk the day after surgery. I've seen kids undergo chemotherapy protocols that would kill an adult—and never miss a day of school. They can smile and joke in the face of pain, and even death.

If you look at this quality of resilience under a microscope, you'll see an extended family of adaptive attributes, some gentle and some fierce. Among the gentler traits that enable children to bend rather than break in a storm are flexibility, resourcefulness, creativity, imagination, and humor. Children's resilience is also abetted by a spectrum of strengths that help them absorb blows to the body and soul and bounce back to vertical, like a bottom-weighted punching bag. These include competitiveness, anger, determination, and tenacity. Finally, there are spiritual attributes that allow children to maintain their equilibrium during a crisis, including hope, faith, trust, and love.

Not every child possesses all of these strengths. But every child—which is to say every one of us when we were young—possesses some of them. As children, we intuited that to survive and thrive we needed to play to the particular strengths that made us resilient. *To the degree that we can continue to access those childhood strengths as adults, we'll be more resilient, more successful, and more fulfilled.*

Before we can access our strengths, we need to first recognize and appreciate them. Playing to strengths sounds obvious, even self-evident, but as a culture we've become hooked on a deficit-based model of identity. We're obsessed with dysfunction and disability; we've become acutely attuned to our fears, our vulnerabilities, and our failings, rather than focusing on our strengths. Whether we're looking at our marriages, our careers, or even our own children, we tend to see deficits rather than assets, limitations rather than potential.

When their children are in mortal peril, many parents recognize that they've been more critical than appreciative of them. A woman named Carrie remembers being very judgmental of her preteen daughter's taste in clothes and music. "Ever since Allie got sick," she says ruefully, "things like wearing tight jeans and tube tops are pretty insignificant. I realize now that listening to Britney Spears won't kill her."

One day, when Carrie and I were watching Allie sleep fitfully in her wheelchair, Carrie confided to me, "I used to be like every other perfectionist parent. I wanted Allie to be a better student, a better musician, whatever it was that would make me prouder to be her mother. It wasn't until she got this tumor that I realized what a miracle she is, and has always been. Now all I want is the chance to keep loving her and to have her in my life."

Another mother, Margaret Rosner, is a very religious woman who nursed her daughter, Sue, through a long series of operations to try to control her malignant brain tumor. Over the course of a decade, from age ten to twenty, Sue gradually lost all of her faculties: first her balance and ability to walk, then her hearing, her sight, and her speech. Throughout Sue's illness, her mother tended to her with infinite care and love.

Margaret never gave in to anger or despair, no matter how much her daughter's tumor took away. As she explained to me near the end of Sue's life, "I believe that God rules the world. I am His daughter, and He loves my daughter, no matter how diminished she becomes. I don't care how she is, as long as she is. Even if she dies, I know that my love for her, and God's love for her, will never end."

It might seem natural for a mother to love her daughter unconditionally. But I think about how habitually most of us find fault with our healthy children. They're not studious enough. They're impolite. They're underachievers. It's easy for us to become so preoccupied with what our children *aren't* that we lose sight of what makes them unique and irreplaceable. We love our children more than life itself, but it's still a struggle to accept them for the flawed and yet perfect individuals they are.

The kids I treat have helped me see straight. Many people look at them and see victims. What I see are kids who have responded to the most extreme circumstances with courage, creativity, and compassion. These young people are exceptional, but they are also human. They suffer from fear and anger and loneliness—and pain across the widest imaginable spectrum. What makes them exceptional is their determination not to let their illness or its stresses rob them of their joy in life. Adversity has held up a mirror to them—and what they've seen is a wealth of inner strengths they had never guessed they possessed.

IN OUR HEARTS, WE WISH CHILDHOOD COULD BE A sanctuary from the trials of adult life. Life teaches us a different truth: that childhood is often the most perilous stage of life. Fortunately, we're a highly adaptive species, and childhood is the most adaptive stage of life. Nature, the Creator, or whatever intelligence guides our evolution, has endowed children with a genius for resilience that can last a lifetime.

One recurrent quality of youthful resilience is being able to bounce back from bad breaks, rather than get stuck in self-pity. We all get unlucky at certain times in our lives. What counts is whether we get hung up on the "Why me?" question or move forward.

Lauren Kathleen Kelley is a master of resilience who refuses to assume the mantle of bad-luck girl. Instead, she's chosen to play to her strengths. She was nine years old when she had the first of five brain surgeries. At seventeen, she now has the wisdom and maturity of a woman twice her age. Here's how she recounts the week her life changed forever: "I always thought that I had the luck of the Irish. But on March 17, 1995—St. Patrick's Day—I was diagnosed with a juvenile pilocytic astrocytoma. In one short week I went from selling Girl Scout cookies and trying out for the softball team to having brain surgery."

Her recovery was grueling. "My rehab was painful and exhausting, but at the end of each day I could breathe a sigh of relief because I knew that I was one step closer to getting my life back." She had to relearn how to walk and talk. She always loved to draw, but for months she could barely hold a pencil. She suffered permanent damage to her optic nerve, causing blurred vision that persists today.

When you ask Lauren about her life, she doesn't dwell on her problems. She prefers to focus on her newfound talents as a problem-solver. She used to read a lot, but because of her vision problems she's learned to become a great listener. Listening to good music has replaced reading a good book. She does her nails under a magnifier and has developed a system for sorting different denominations of bills in her wallet. Her loss of mobility and balance has made her more aware of what's going on around her; now that she's not in such a rush, she's become more observant of her surroundings.

Lauren used to take things for granted. Now she values every day, takes satisfaction in every achievement. "I realize that with all I've lost, I have gained a lot too," she says. "I know that I am one of the lucky ones. I'm a survivor."

This extraordinarily poised teenager was invited to cross

the country and address an audience of senators and congress-people on Capitol Hill during Brain Tumor Awareness Week last year. "I didn't get nervous until I found out I was speaking right after Hillary Clinton and just before AOL chairman Steve Case," she says with a giggle. "But it worked out all right. I was able to pick up a lot of public speaking tips just by watching Hillary. Simple things like making eye contact and speaking slowly. I did fine. When Steve Case began his speech by saying, 'Lauren, you're a tough act to follow,' everyone laughed and clapped. Afterwards, a senator said to me, 'Everyone in this room fell in love with you.' I did feel a lot of love coming at me while I was speaking. Maybe it was because my parents and brothers were sitting in the front row."

For Lauren, it's the small, personal victories that have meant the most. Every summer since she was a kid, Lauren's family has spent August at a lake in the Adirondack Mountains. Her favorite pastime used to be water-skiing, and ever since her surgery, getting back up on her skis became Lauren's benchmark for recovery. She had promised herself that she wasn't going to let her brain tumor keep her from doing the things she loved, and water skiing was definitely her greatest love.

The first summer she tried, she was overwhelmed with nervousness while her mother helped her on with the skis. Her father sat in the boat with her brother, Reed. She got into position in the water, her knees up against her chest and her hands grasping the towrope in front of her. Her father waited for her to get steady. Then her brother yelled, "Are you ready?" Lauren took a deep breath and answered, "I guess so." He father revved the engine into forward, Lauren rose up on her skis—and crashed face-first into the water.

That's pretty much how it went for the next two summers. She never lacked for heart, but whatever mix of balance and strength she needed eluded her. It was frustrating because her body could remember how it felt to glide across the surface of the water, skimming in wide arcs behind the boat as her brother cheered her on. But somewhere in her brain the wires were crossed.

Finally, last summer, she felt strong and confident. "The whole time I was putting on my vest and skis, I kept trying to think of something to motivate and inspire me. When I grabbed the towline and gave my father the thumbs-up sign, for some reason Derek Jeter came into my head. I don't know why, except that he's my favorite baseball player. So I closed my eyes and saw Derek crouching at shortstop, ready for whatever might come his way. I heard the motor get louder and I gritted my teeth and opened my eyes. The boat pulled me up out of the water, and I got to the spot where I usually fell on my face—and that's when I pulled back on the line with all my strength and I stayed up. Reed was whooping in the back of the boat and I could hear cheers from the beach behind me. I was on top of the world. I stayed there for three minutes, until I tried to cut across my wake and wiped out. Next year I'll make that turn."

ONE SHARED TRAIT AMONG MY MOST RESILIENT YOUNG patients is an ability to accept help. It's a paradox: those who have trouble accepting the help they need get discouraged and depressed. Those who can accept help without shame are the ones who become more self-reliant.

Getting past the shame of needing help is key. My patients' ability to prevail over their medical condition has less to do with the degree of their physical deficit than with their optimism and their underlying self-esteem. Some people who make dramatic physical recoveries never get over the feeling of being damaged goods. Others get worse rather than better physically, but emotionally they're able to transcend the limitations of their bodies.

Stella Wainwright is a girl who's blessed with a remarkably transcendent spirit. By any objective measure, she's had a terrible time of it. She's suffered from hydrocephalous since infancy, with a host of complications that often accompany this disorder. By the time she was a teenager she'd had meningitis, a stroke, and multiple shunts implanted to drain fluid from her brain.

Stella's character strengths are equal to her numerous afflictions. She's got a great sense of humor. She's determined and hardworking. And she's never felt sorry for herself. Despite her ongoing medical problems, she was always a good student, and she graduated from college with honors.

She had begun graduate studies toward a degree in social work when her body presented her with a new, even more daunting challenge: she contracted arachnoiditis, a neurological disease that caused her hands to clench and her legs to become spastic. Gradually her arms and legs wasted away to the point where she couldn't walk.

She was understandably depressed and confused about how her life would continue. But since she'd been dealing with health problems all her life, she'd also developed powerful coping skills. Stella remembers her dramatic and unexpected psychological breakthrough: "Though my physical condition was progressively deteriorating, I received the most amazing gift I could ever imagine. Gradually, my confusion began to disappear and was replaced by a feeling of wonder at the journey I was embarked on. Despite my physical decline, my spirit had never felt more alive. I knew I didn't really have any control over my medical problems. They would always have their own timetable. But I *could* control my response to my illness. No matter how bad my physical problems became, I knew I would never lose control over who I was and how I responded."

Stella realized that whether or not she was capable of walking or caring for herself independently, she would be strong enough to handle the changes she might have to face. She was fortunate to have a family that would always be there for her. "But other people can't rescue you from depression or confusion," she says. "God isn't going to appear and reveal why these things are happening to you. There's a point at which you have to save yourself."

This was a profound epiphany for Stella. "What it feels like to me is that my mind just took over for everything that my body couldn't handle. It didn't matter whether I could take care of myself physically. So long as I was able to take care of myself emotionally, as long as I could handle what was going on without panicking or blaming someone or feeling sorry for myself, I knew I'd be all right. Even when I couldn't dress myself because my hands were clenched so badly, I never felt helpless."

It's scary to admit that you need help. Particularly in a culture that promotes rugged individualism and self-reliance as its loftiest ideals. I'm a big believer in self-reliance; unless you believe that you can take care of yourself you can never take care of someone else. But true self-reliance means soliciting and accepting support when you need it, appreciating your strengths, while not denying your weaknesses.

Accepting help while pursuing self-reliance is a tricky dance. All children struggle to stay in step as they're growing up. They crave their parents' love and support; and they crave independence with equal measure. When they grow up, many adults transfer their conflicted drives for dependence and self-reliance to their marriages. They want their spouse to take care of them, but they want to keep their autonomy intact. Regardless of the stage of life, the challenge remains the same: How do you accommodate your weaknesses so you can exploit your strengths?

If I hadn't accepted the help I was offered as a child—by my aunt, my fifth-grade teacher, my psychiatrist, and my father—I'd never have made it to medical school. Not being afraid to ask for help has made a huge difference to my career. Many professionals, as they become more accomplished and senior in their positions, grow fearful of admitting their weaknesses and soliciting help. They're afraid it will undermine other people's respect for their abilities. Or they fear that by inviting talented people to support them, they may be shown up.

I always tried to be pragmatic about who I needed to help me get the job done, and then I recruited these people to the task. When I moved to Beth Israel, I especially looked for surgeons who were strong in areas where I wasn't. One of the junior surgeons on my staff is technically more accomplished than I am. There are certain tumor removals that involve complex spatial relationships between nerves and arteries that I've never felt fully confident in attacking, and I'm only too happy to have him take those cases. Another surgeon has a particularly good rapport with teenagers. Yet another surgeon is masterful inside the spinal cord. I always figure that when the people I mentor surpass me, they make me look good.

Because I want to make the most of my God-given strengths,

I've learned not to fear having my weaknesses exposed. I've always been highly functional in certain fairly narrow areas, and hopeless in others. I've had attention problems all my life; I can hyperfocus in the operating room, but otherwise I'm all over the place. I can't stand still and I'm lousy at keeping track of things. I'm good with patients and their families, but I can't bear to sit through administrative meetings. As a parent, I was better at playing with my kids than I was at giving them limits or discipline. I mostly wanted to spoil them.

To compensate for my weaknesses, I've always allied myself with strong women. They've been my anchors at work and in my home life. My wife, Kathy, was only eighteen when I met her, but I immediately recognized her strengths of character and will, and I understood that those qualities would make her a great partner. I knew I needed someone who was smart, self-confident, and unflappable—particularly in ways that I wasn't. Some people might say that Kathy has indulged my childlike qualities while being the necessary grown-up in our family. If so, I only hope I've enabled her happiness as much as she has mine.

At the hospital I've always relied on similarly strong women to give me support and guidance. The neurosurgical community is still virtually an all-boys club, but the people who've made my medical world function have almost all been women. Tania Maher, our head triage nurse, is the best diagnostician at the INN. I trust her instincts and her judgment above anyone else's. She's loyal to her patients and she's tough as nails—not in the macho way that surgeons play tough, but in a results-oriented style that gets her patients what they need when they need it, no matter how many rules have to be bent, egos bruised, or hospital bureaucrats finessed.

Tania's style of tough is emblematic of what I've come to prize and protect in our nursing staff. I've always felt that good nurses are a lot harder to find and keep than good surgeons. Surgeons get the high profiles and the big salaries, but it's the nurses who heal the hurts. Long after the surgeons have gone home to bed, the nurses are still at the hospital safeguarding their patients, body and soul.

I THINK THAT ANGER HAS GOTTEN SHORT SHRIFT AS AN adaptive trait, and that acceptance is overrated as a virtue. At critical times in my life, anger has served me well. Acceptance has never been my strong suit. I've never accepted kids dying. I've never accepted the term "inoperable" when it came to a child's brain tumor. I never accepted the widely held belief that I couldn't become a doctor. When the NYU medical school dean blew me off I resolved to get my medical degree any way and anywhere I could—so I could shove it in his face.

Anger is useful—to a point. Eventually, it outlives its usefulness and becomes a trap; it's a lot easier to stay angry than to get over it. Anger can be an effective shield and a weapon.

But it can also become a clunky suit of armor that only serves to keep other people out. My most resilient patients realize that until they lay down their sword and shield of anger, they can't retrieve the trust they discarded along the way.

Beginning at the age of six, Brian McNair suffered from crushing daily headaches. His mother had always had been afflicted by migraines, so everyone thought Brian had inherited the problem. The pain was excruciating; "like a rain of bombs going off in my head" is how Brian described them. He threw up most mornings, and he spent half his time at school lying down in the nurse's office.

Years went by and his headaches continued. Brian became a social outcast, a boy who couldn't have a normal childhood because he wasn't able to do the usual boy things. He was the kid who was always sick, who couldn't go on sleepovers, who couldn't play contact sports. We don't like to face up to how cruel children can be to one another, but anyone who stands out as different in grade school or high school is likely to become a target. The other boys teased Brian and bullied him mercilessly. As the torment and abuse at school persisted, he withdrew into his private world of pain. His only refuge was swimming. He was always a strong swimmer, and something about moving through the water was physically and emotionally comforting to him.

His mother took him to headache specialists and psychiatrists and neurologists. No one could find an organic cause for his headaches. Brian got one of those nondiagnosis diagnoses, what doctors call "idiopathic pain," which translates into plain English as "despite all our technology and fancy degrees, we can't figure out why you hurt." The only medications that relieved Brian's pain were opiates that knocked him out.

By the time he got to junior high school, Brian's classmates had officially labeled him "the freak," and his tormentors ratcheted up their intimidation and threats. He was reluctant to log on to his e-mail for fear of what he'd find there. Finally, at the age of fourteen, Brian reached the end of his tether. His anger at his tormentors turned in on himself. "I would walk along the tracks near my house and think about throwing myself in front of the next train," he recalls. "I came to the point where I threw up my hands and decided that only God could save me."

When Brian confided his suicidal thoughts to his mother, she took him to the hospital and insisted they perform another series of brain scans. His MRI revealed a golf ball–sized tumor pressing against the pain center of his brain. His doctor suggested he come to New York for treatment.

Surgery turned out to be the simplest part of Brian's recovery. His tumor was removed without any problems. Two days after his operation, Brian's headaches went away and never returned. Brian and his mother were ecstatic. Finally, he could have a normal life!

But eight years of physical and emotional pain don't heal

overnight. His first encounter with the trials of reentry occurred at the airport on his way home. Two weeks after surgery, he still had half his head shaved with stitches down the side of his scalp. He looked so scary—"like Frankenstein's ugly brother," recalls Brian—that the airline wouldn't let him board the plane. He had to wait in the passenger lounge until we faxed a letter from the hospital assuring them that he was well enough to fly. "Just as I was starting my new life," he says, "I felt like a freak all over again."

His physical scars soon healed, but the emotional scars of his eight-year ordeal were just coming into view. Brian's parents had moved to a new home in a new school district so he'd have a fresh start in high school. But Brian quickly realized that during all those years when he was battling his headaches, other kids were growing up, making friends, and establishing trusting relationships. Brian had felt betrayed by every friend he'd ever made.

He was antisocial and shy. Most of all he was angry. Why wasn't brain surgery enough to make him well? Why hadn't stopping the pain in his head soothed the hurt in his heart? What had he ever done to deserve the cruel torment he'd endured?

When people extended their hand in friendship, Brian withdrew his in distrust. If a girl looked at him with interest, he was convinced she was staring at his scar. Even though he was a stranger in his new school, he felt that everyone knew that he was different. And in truth, he *was* different. He'd never had a best friend. He'd never felt the trust and affection of a buddy, much less a girlfriend. He'd never been part of a team.

It wasn't until tenth grade that he felt brave enough to put his feelings on the line. The school was offering an elective course in architectural drafting—a subject that combined his longtime interest in drawing and in building things. He'd always had trouble with math, though, and he was worried about handling the quantitative material in the course. His drafting partner, Matt, turned out to be another shy kid. Working side by side and collaborating on an elaborate drafting project together, they became close friends. "We were like brothers" says Brian. "We still are." In that same class Brian was blessed with a teacher who recognized his special talents and encouraged him to develop them.

"Finding a friend—a real soul mate—and having a teacher who believed in me really opened up my world," Brian explains. "Before that, I was like a clam with my shell clamped shut. As soon as I unclenched just a little, the whole world came pouring in." He became a hardworking student, and he sprinted to catch up with his classmates outside of school—making friends, going to parties, going out on dates. He met a girl and risked his heart on her. "She was much too pretty for a guy like me," he says, "but big surprise—she didn't seem to think so!"

This fall Brian is going to a top-flight college to pursue a career as an architect. Brian's still not "normal"—he's endured too much to ever be as innocent as a typical eighteen-year-old. But he's not afraid to trust people anymore. "I still have a scar running down the side of my head," he tells me. "When I meet someone I like, one of the first things I do is part my hair to show them the 'before and after' dividing line in my life. I want them to know that I'm not just anybody—that if I weren't such a strong person, I wouldn't be here."

I've seen a lot of my patients live out the same kind of Ugly Duckling drama that Brian and I went through: the kid who's different from the others, who's teased and humiliated, who has to endure a long cold winter before the spring comes—and with it the salvation of a newborn adult identity. Once you've been an ugly duckling, you never forget what it feels like to be an outsider. Even after you've taken your rightful place among your fellow swans, part of you will always feel like an odd duck—and you'll always feel for the other ugly ducklings who still don't have a flock to call their own.

I DON'T KNOW MUCH ABOUT HEAVEN. I DON'T KNOW whether it's a place we go to or come from, or if it only exists inside the fleeting moments of joy life grants us from time to time. For me, heaven is being in a boat on the water. Any boat on any water. It's where I've always felt happiest and most at peace, ever since I was a boy. It's where I can be alone without feeling lonely, adrift without feeling lost.

Hell is something I'm more knowledgeable about. I've seen it all too often through the eyes of mothers and fathers of sick kids. I've seen it on their faces as they try to make their child's pain go away, in their clenched jaws as they struggle to stay strong for their son or to somehow not go to pieces in front of their daughter, because they know that's their impossible job.

My personal hell is watching a child's life slip away, despite everything I'm trying to do to save him. It's the loneliest, most wretched feeling in my world. When a kid I'm treating dies, I'm always shattered, no matter how many times it's happened in the past. I always blame myself. I wonder if I could have been more creative or resourceful. To be honest, I can't remember all the names and faces of the kids who get well and grow up. But the ones who die I still see in my dreams.

When I'm stuck in my hell, or see patients and families mired in theirs, I remember Winston Churchill's advice: "When you're going through hell, keep going." There's no clearly marked exit sign in hell, and there's only one direction leading out—which is forward.

Prevailing over serious illness, or any severe adversity, requires tenacity. I'm in awe of how my patients and their families keep on going through hell until they come out on the other side. They are fighters who never say die.

Tory Wachtel is one of them. He was only nineteen months old when he was diagnosed with a rare type of tumor in his brain stem. His first doctors told his parents that Tory wouldn't make it—no one else with this kind of tumor ever had. When he became my patient I had only operated on a handful of other tumors like his, and the chemotherapy protocol was a virtual blank slate.

So we made it up as we went along. I operated. Twice. We came up with a chemo protocol. We held our breath.

We must have done something right because Tory went into remission for five years. He was a bright kid—he learned to read before kindergarten and by first grade it was clear that he was gifted in math. Then his tumor grew back.

The next eighteen months were very rough. Tory was in a lot of pain, and his body was getting weaker and weaker. We tried surgery and chemo and more surgery and steroids, but his tumor from hell kept growing back. Tory was constantly in and out of the hospital—and he kept bouncing back. If I told Tory he'd have to recuperate in the hospital for five days after surgery, he'd make sure he was out in three. In between surgeries, Tory went back to school to be with his classmates. After his final craniotomy at the age of eight, he didn't get back to class until the last day of second grade. But he still wanted to be there to say good-bye to his teachers and friends before summer vacation.

Meanwhile, Tory's parents had to figure out how to keep on going with little hope to cling to. During Tory's first round of surgeries, his mother, Linda, gave birth to a boy with a severe genetic disorder. He only lived for seven months. Linda remembers, "All I really wanted to do was crawl into bed and stay there." Instead, she forced herself to be optimistic. Her goal became to preserve whatever normalcy she could in Tory's life, and in their family's. "I wanted him to have a childhood, no matter how short it might turn out to be." They took a trip to Disneyland. They adopted a baby girl. And they waited for daylight.

Linda came up with a metaphor to explain the painful trial-and-error treatment regimen to Tory, and to herself. "It's like a jigsaw puzzle. You have to try this piece and that piece, and if you're patient enough, eventually you'll find the piece that makes all the other pieces fit together." When Tory asked her, "What happens if they don't find the piece that gets me better?" she told him, "They will."

Each therapy had bought us some time, but time was running out. It wasn't until we were out of options and out of time that we finally found the missing piece. As a last-ditch effort, we decided to try radiation. It could have caused life-threatening complications, but it didn't. It shouldn't have worked on his type of tumor, but it did.

Tory was back in school a week after radiation therapy. His MRI scans have been clean ever since. Now he's sixteen and learning to drive like everyone else in his class. "At least now I have something else to worry about," Linda jokes.

Tory has more problems to contend with than most teenagers. He has some facial paralysis that makes one eye droop, and his smile looks crooked. But he's a lot more self-confident and less self-conscious than most adolescents. If you ask him, he'll tell you, "I look fine. I can live with it." He has some learning disabilities, but he's outstanding at math. His parents have worked with his school to develop a teaching plan that plays to his strengths, and he gets A's and B's in all his courses. His balance and coordination aren't great, but that hasn't kept him from playing basketball and baseball and soccer.

Perhaps the bravest decision Tory made was to run for president of his eighth-grade class. Anyone who's survived middle school remembers how cruel and unusually punishing kids this age can be. Running for class president might seem masochistic under the best of circumstances. Tory wasn't fazed.

"The other candidates are running on really idiotic platforms," he explained to his mother one afternoon. "They say they'll abolish homework and get us a shorter school week. I have some good ideas, some real issues. Better food in the cafeteria, and getting weekly homework assignments posted on the Internet. I'm going to run."

"Are you sure you want to?" his mother asked, cringing inside at her own memories of eighth grade.

"If I win, I win. If I lose, I lose. I want to do it."

So he did. He recruited campaign aides who helped him distribute leaflets and posters. He posted his platform on his website. He lobbied for votes in the lunchroom. He made a campaign speech in front of 250 classmates.

Five kids ran for president. Tory came in second, four votes behind the winner.

In ninth grade his English teacher assigned everyone an essay topic: Write about the essence of who you are. Tory wrote: "When people look at me, they see me as a person who's been sick. That's not the essence of who I am. I'm a normal kid who's had a normal life, except when I was having surgery. My tumor never touched my essence, because it never stopped me from doing what I wanted to do."

My guess is that Tory will keep on doing what he wants to do for a very long time. He reminds me of that other dogged fighter, Winston Churchill, who struggled mightily against learning disabilities in his youth and wrote of his school days, "It was not pleasant to feel oneself so completely outclassed and left behind at the beginning of the race." Like Churchill, Tory refused to be left behind and refused to drop out of the race. Instead, he outran his tumor, and kept on going.

6

Love Without Boundaries

Now I know I've got a heart, because it's breaking.

—The Tin Woodman in *The Wizard of Oz*

Unconditional love. It's what we all search for, from cradle to grave. As children, we yearn for it from our parents. On our wedding day, we pledge it to our spouse. When we become parents, we feel it viscerally when our children cling to us, and we to them. Instinctively, we return their love— until they start to talk back or fail to meet our expectations.

We all wish to love and be loved without boundaries, but human love seems to exist perpetually in a land of "if." If you love me back. If you make me happy. If you make me proud. If I can be the boss. If I don't change my mind. By the time we grow up, our hearts are walled in by distrust and fear: fear of betrayal, of abandonment, of death. No wonder true love is the mainstay of fairy tales and romantic fiction; it's so rare in real life.

I think love is so challenging and humbling because it calls on all our strengths: kindness, courage, faith, tenacity, resilience, and, most of all, the ability to live emotionally in the moment. None of us is playing with a full deck in this regard, though some of us were dealt better hands than others.

Children are blessed with an innate mastery of love; they're wired by evolution to express and attract it for the sake of their own survival. Children also have the advantage of limited personal history. Because they're young and haven't had their hearts broken, they can play at love. They can be fearless.

My first experience of unconditional love was with my dachshund, Skipper, my best friend between the ages of eight and twelve. Skipper had all the classic canine virtues: he was a good listener, a faithful companion, and endlessly affectionate. It's easy to love a dog, and I imagine it must be easy for a dog to love a boy. In my child's world of conflicted emotions, where I always felt judged and I never felt I was measuring up, the love I felt for and from Skipper was simple and pure. I've had dogs in my life ever since.

As a young man I hoped to find unconditional love in the arms of a perfect girlfriend. Instead, I got my heart bruised and broken. I discovered that romantic love was intensely emotional, but hardly unconditional. Even inside a happy marriage to Kathy, I learned that love only works in combination with compromise and perseverance.

It wasn't until I started working with kids, and had children of my own, that I experienced unconditional love. Arriving home from work I would be greeted by an excited chorus of "Daddy, Daddy!" along with the pure rush of exuberant hugs. Meanwhile, the seriously sick children I was treating at the hospital showed me love uninhibited by fear. I'd see them comfort one another with love. I'd see how their love inspired their parents to unbelievable feats of emotional stamina and melted the hearts of battled-hardened surgeons and oncologists. I'd see how it silenced the voice that echoes in the heart of every doctor and nurse who works around very sick children—the voice that asks: Do I dare get close to this little boy? Should I risk my heart on this little girl?

Children's genius for love is not a cultural trait. I've treated kids from India and China, from Israel and Jordan, from South America and the South Bronx. They're all the same at heart. They're all exceptional because they make us dig and dig until we uncover the best in ourselves. They make us find our courage, and the outer reaches of our love.

FAMILY IS THE TESTING GROUND OF LOVE. IT'S WHERE we first learn the rules, where we fail and succeed at love, often within the same day. Family is where we look for love when we're up against the ropes with nowhere else to turn.

When we refer to functional and dysfunctional families, we're really talking about how freely love is passed around and how efficiently the reservoir of love is refilled. A child's illness is the ultimate test of how a family functions in crisis. Some pass and some fail. What I've learned from close observation is just how resilient an organism a family can be. Even in the worst crisis, the strong families manage to uncover hidden reserves of love, like secret wells in a seemingly arid desert.

Tensions between mothers and their teenage daughters and between fathers and their sons are legendary, the stuff of classic drama and television melodrama. But in the midst of trauma, I've seen parents and their children forge unbreakable bonds of love.

"Up until December 21, 1997, our family was busy preparing for the holidays, raising our family, and trying to accumulate the things that we thought we needed to be happy." That's how Ellen Simms begins the story of her family's harrowing trip into illness. And here's her ending: "The things that were important to us five years ago are no longer important. We've learned to live one day at a time and to appreciate the truly important things in life . . . each other." The middle chapters are a lot less tidy.

Just before Christmas five years ago, Ellen's thirteen-year-old daughter, Cynthia, had a grand mal seizure that was caused by a benign brain tumor. I was able to remove it without incident, and Cynthia was soon back at school and getting on with her life.

As scary as her brain tumor was, the Simms family didn't start to unravel until a month after Cynthia's return to school, when Ellen was diagnosed with stage 2 breast cancer. While Ellen underwent surgery, chemotherapy, and radiation, Cynthia had to become the mother of the household. She had to get her younger sister, Melanie, off to school every morning, and she had to shop for and cook dinner each night, since her father worked long hours and spent his spare time tending to his wife.

Ellen thought the way her daughter took on so many adult responsibilities was heroic. "I was scared out my wits by my cancer," she recounts. "Cynthia's bravery was my inspiration to keep on fighting." But it was more than Cynthia was prepared to handle as a thirteen-year-old. Her mother's illness was scarier for her than her own medical crisis had been. "If you die, you don't have to worry," Cynthia explains. "But if your mom dies, you have to deal with it forever."

Cynthia's anxiety soon turned to anger toward Ellen. "I hated that she wasn't there as my mother," she says now, as she prepares to head off to college. "And I hated having to take care of my sister and father, instead of being taken care of." She and her mother fought a lot during that period, and they both felt guilty afterward. "We said terrible things to each other," says Cynthia. "It seemed like we never talked—we only shouted."

What Cynthia didn't know at the time was that her mother was battling more than cancer. In the months following her surgery, Ellen became addicted to medication she had been prescribed following her surgery. At the same time, she began drinking heavily. As the months passed, and Ellen became more and more dependent on alcohol and pills, she realized that she was in deep trouble. But she was too ashamed to turn to her husband for help. All Cynthia knew was that her mother was sleeping much of the day, and when she was awake she seemed to be yelling at her a lot.

Things came to a head a year later on Mother's Day. The extended family went out to a fancy restaurant to celebrate, and Cynthia walked into the ladies' room to find that her mother had passed out on the floor from pills and drink. When Cynthia came home from school the next day, her mother and father sat her down and told her the truth. Ellen was an alcoholic and addict who was going to need help to get well. Cynthia took the news hard. "Those two words— alcoholic and addict—didn't apply to my family. We lived in a middle-class neighborhood in Connecticut. In my mind alcoholics were homeless slobbering men. Not my mother, who just 'liked to sleep a lot.'"

When Ellen tried to stop on her own, cold turkey, the sudden withdrawal sent her body into violent seizures. Her husband rushed her to the emergency room. For the first time, Cynthia saw her mother as someone who was sick, as someone who was struggling to recover and survive. "That wasn't just the turning point of my relationship with my mother," says Cynthia, "but the turning point of my life so far."

In the months that followed, Ellen and Cynthia became each other's closest friend and ally. The anger seeped away and was replaced by trust. Ellen has been in recovery from alcoholism and drug addiction for more than three years. She's worked hard to stay sober and to rebuild her relationship with her older daughter. "Making amends is a big part of any 12-step program," says Ellen today. "I've learned that the best way to make amends is to be a loving, supportive mother. I'm amazed at what wonderful girls I have in spite of all they've been through. I can't believe it sometimes, but Cynthia and I have the closest relationship of any mother and daughter I know."

"Sometimes the worst of situations produce the best results," says Cynthia. "Now that my mother and I have been through this together, I can see that she's not just a strong woman and an amazing mother, but also my best friend. Until the day I die she'll be my hero."

TEENAGE BOYS ARE NOTORIOUSLY WITHDRAWN AND SELF-conscious around their parents. One of the unforeseen by-products of serious illness is how it forces boys to confront emotions that most teenagers, and many adults, work hard to avoid.

Bill Kassen was an eighteen-year-old jock from Staten Island. He excelled at football and hockey and learned to play through pain without complaint. When he came into the INN for brain surgery, he put on a brave front. When his teammates came to visit the afternoon before his operation, he laughed and joked with them. But then they left, and Bill was left alone with his fears. That night, Bill was in a lot of pain because we'd had to suspend his narcotic pain medication twelve hours before surgery. Pain has a way of slowing down time, just when you most want to speed it up. But it was fear as much as the physical pain that drove Bill to the brink of panic that night.

"My mom and dad were there in my hospital room with me," he recalls. "I'd never really lost it in front of them—not since I was a kid. But having them there with me late at night, I felt okay about breaking down and crying. So I did. I cried and cried. They each held one of my hands and said it would be okay, and that I had every right to feel bad. Mostly, though, it was just having them there and knowing that they loved me that made everything all right. It felt good to let it all out, all the fear that had been building up inside me for weeks. I learned something that night that I never knew before—letting yourself go to pieces in front of people you trust, people who love you, is sometimes the best thing you can do for yourself."

Another teenage patient of mine, Jason North, was a freshman at Harvard when an MRI revealed that the source of his back pain was a foot-long tumor in his spine. He and his father arrived in New York two days before surgery, with too much time on their hands and not enough to do. Jason was scared. He realized that he might die. "I thought about all the things I could have done, but hadn't," he says. "I thought about every time I could have taken a walk around the block with my father, but passed up the opportunity for one reason or another. Now everything was suddenly different, in a very frightening way. It felt like my life was slipping away from me."

The night before his surgery Jason and his father were staying at a hotel in midtown. After dinner and a ballgame on television, Jason was too anxious to sleep, so his father stayed up with him. Despite his back pain, Jason wanted to walk, so all night they walked and talked. Not about serious stuff, just anything that would take Jason's mind off the next morning. They talked about baseball and Boston and music and girls and how bad the food was at college. They walked all the way down Broadway to the financial district. Then they headed north again. At three in the morning, when the streets finally became deserted, his father thought they should go inside. Jason still didn't want to go to bed, so they walked in circles around the spacious hotel lobby for another couple of hours. At dawn, they took a cab uptown to the hospital.

There are basically two kinds of problems I deal with as a surgeon: those I can fix, and those I can't. Jason's was one that I could fix. He was lucky—and his good fortune wasn't lost on him. He spent the two weeks following surgery getting back on his feet and hanging around with the other children on the unit. They were mostly younger and sicker than he was. "I realized that many of those kids would probably never make it," he says. "They'd never hear their first high-school bell. Never play a game of intramural basketball. Never sneak into an R-rated movie. I felt I owed it to them to treat every single day as a gift and a privilege."

When Jason went back to school, he was no longer the world-weary college freshman. "I began appreciating things anew," he says. "The food didn't taste so bad. Listening to a live concert wasn't just a good time, it was a wonder. And I started to see that a good friend isn't just a person you get along with, but another soul who changes yours forever. I realized my dad was one of my soulmates."

SIBLING RELATIONSHIPS, FOR BETTER OR WORSE, NEVER go away. You can't divorce your brother or sister. They're the first people you compete with for love and attention, and they're usually destined to share more of life's milestones with you than your spouse will. Who else remembers what you wore on Halloween when you were six? And who else saw your parents kissing or fighting? For all the inherent rivalry between siblings, they can also be one another's lifeline in a crisis.

Brianna Reed and her twin sister, Sarah, taught me a lot about love without boundaries. I had to operate on Brianna three days before her thirteenth birthday. You'd think turning thirteen in a hospital room with your head still in bandages would be the most depressing way imaginable to become a teenager. But according to Brianna, it was one of her best birthdays ever. Her sister made sure of it.

All morning, while Brianna was in physiotherapy, Sarah decorated her sister's room. She got so dizzy from blowing up balloons she had to lie down on Brianna's bed. When Brianna returned at lunchtime, she couldn't tell it was a hospital room. Every surface was covered with blue and pink streamers—even the IV poles were wrapped like candy canes.

Sarah had brought Brianna a party dress from home—the one she knew she'd want to wear. She helped her sister dress, then carefully applied makeup to cover the places around her eyes that were still black from surgery. Finally, Sarah produced a hat of her own that Brianna always admired, and secured it gently over her bandages.

By late afternoon the room was crammed with family, friends, and staff. It was so crowded you could hardly move in there. In the middle of the crush was Brianna, opening presents and giggling excitedly like any thirteen-year-old birthday girl. Then someone doused the lights and Sarah stepped forward holding a cake and candles.

Today, as a fifteen-year-old high-school sophomore, Brianna still shakes her head in amazement at the memory of that moment. "It wasn't until everyone was singing 'Happy

Birthday' and I was about to blow out the candles that I suddenly realized what was wrong with this picture. It was Sarah's birthday too! She had spent her whole birthday planning my party and making sure I had a good time—but she was turning thirteen that day also. I was about to wish that I'd be around for my sixteenth birthday, which would be my next big one. But then I stopped and made a different wish: that I would be as good a sister to Sarah as she'd been to me. We still fight all the time, and she still wears my clothes and forgets to return them about six times a week. But I'll always remember that when I needed it the most, my sister put me first. She gave me a present that day that I'll never forget."

AMONG ALL OUR FEARS, OUR FEAR OF DEATH IS THE MOST powerful. Death is so scary that we deny its hovering presence in our lives. In reality, death is our constant companion; its proximity is part of what makes life so glorious. To me, suffering is the ultimate evil, not death. Love is the ultimate good, because it outlasts suffering, and even death.

All parents are devastated by the death of a child. The pain never goes away. But I've seen many remarkable families transform their personal catastrophe into a blessing for other children. When a child's love takes root in a parent's heart, it can bring forth new life.

Kyle Brice was single when she conceived Andrew, and

many people discouraged her from trying to raise a child alone. She never regretted the decision to keep her son, even when Andrew was diagnosed with brain cancer at the age of seven. "I experienced the miracle of life looking at and touching my son for the first time," she says. "When Andrew was wheeled into surgery the first time, I learned the meaning of prayer."

Over the course of the next four years, Andrew displayed a combination of courage and compassion that inspired all of us, especially his mother. When they stayed at the Ronald McDonald house with other families awaiting surgery, Andrew was constantly approaching other kids and their parents to comfort and reassure them. Andrew battled valiantly against his disease until it took his life at the age of eleven. "I called him Andrew the Warrior, because he was always ready to fight," Kyle recalls. "He was a special child, and he had become a man by the time he left."

The summer before Andrew died, he and Kyle visited the Alamo in San Antonio, Texas. Andrew and Kyle were both moved by how the spirit of that doomed fort spoke to their increasingly dire situation. "Even when you're outnumbered by adversaries ten to one," Kyle explains, "even when they're taking no prisoners and they're pouring over the walls, within your soul you still have options. You can decide that here is where you will stand, that here is where you will draw the line. The message we both took away from the Alamo was:

There is such as thing as victory in death. If you live with a sense of purpose, your spirit will survive you."

A few months after their trip, Andrew had a recurrence and was facing yet another operation. His entire extended family was moping around the house, feeling miserable. Andrew went upstairs and returned carrying a box of "Remember the Alamo" pins he'd bought at the fort. He walked around the living room, fastening a pin onto each person's collar.

After Andrew died, Kyle was a wreck. What kept her going were all the vivid memories of Andrew's courage and kindness. Once, while Andrew had suffered through a cycle of chemotherapy without complaint, Kyle had said to him, "You deserve a medal." Andrew's face brightened at the notion. "You think so?" he had responded. Now that he was gone, Kyle wanted to find a way to keep Andrew's fighting spirit alive and to honor other children's bravery.

So six months after Andrew's death, Kyle founded a non-profit group called Andrew's Warriors. Its mission is to return the smiles and laughter to the lives of children in medical crisis. One of its ongoing activities is to recognize the valor of kids who are fighting against deadly disease by giving them medals. "Kids get medals for athletic achievement and for winning spelling bees," explains Kyle. "Don't the bravest kids in the world deserve some recognition? People think of these kids as victims. To me, they're heroes and they're fighters who never say die. Giving these children medals is such a simple thing, but it works wonders. You should see the way their eyes light up and their chests puff out with pride. Every time we give a child a medal and I see him or her smile, I see Andrew smile."

Andrew's life was brief and his death defies explanation. But the valor he displayed now resonates in the lives of the children who need it most. Kyle and the people who support Andrew's Warriors have created a chain reaction of love and determination that will continue indefinitely. "What Andrew taught me is that our time here is so fleeting—just a moment really," says Kyle. "Unless we are doing things based on an eternal perspective, we will always long for fulfillment. Andrew always seemed to recognize that his days were numbered, but that his soul existed in eternity. Whenever I said to him, 'I love you,' he always responded, 'I love you too, Mommy. To infinity.'"

A FEW YEARS AGO, I HAD A VISIT FROM A COUPLE I HAD never met before. Twelve years earlier when I was at NYU, Linda and Carlo Schejola had sent me films of their young son's brain tumor, and I had advised them over the phone about his treatment options. It was the sort of phone consultation I conducted several times a week; I didn't even remember the conversation until they reminded me. Their son, Micól, eventually died, but they told me that our phone call had been hugely comforting to them at a difficult time. They had promised themselves that if they ever had the means, they would do something to help other children and other families.

Then the Schejolas explained that they had recently sold their family business, and they wanted to make a gift of two million dollars to our unit.

While the Schejolas' gift was unusually generous, many parents of children who have been treated at the INN have been moved to help other children. Once people have shared the experience of nursing a very sick child, they truly become one another's family—the same way that any family bonds around adversity. Regardless of a child's medical outcome, healing is an ongoing process that we go through together, a continuum that doesn't end when a child is cured, that doesn't end when a child dies.

Once a year we hold a memorial service to commemorate the children who died on our unit. Families of all religions come together with our medical staff to pray and to remember the blessings of each child's life and spirit. It's important for all of us—parents, families, and our medical staff—to remember each child as an individual who touched our souls and who is still part of our lives. We light candles for each child and share memories of things they said and did that changed us. We say prayers and sing and cry. The words and tears can't fill the hole left by the children who are no longer with us. But it's a start.

The Angel Book is part of our remembrance, an album that commemorates the children who died on the unit that year. Each child is memorialized with photographs and the fond recollections of staff and family. Among the children remembered in one of our first Angel Books was Allison Trunz. "Up until the day Allison was diagnosed with a brain tumor at the age of three," wrote her mother, Jeannie, "I had every reason to believe that I was raising a child for greatness. That day was the beginning of a nightmare from which I felt I'd never awaken."

Allison led her parents through that dark time and helped them enjoy simple pleasures made timeless by her company. Feeding Cheerios to a chipmunk with Allison in the backyard became a source of amazement to them. So did a walk along the beach. When she was at the INN for treatment, Allison would explore the outer reaches of the hospital with her father, Greg. Once, when it snowed, they sneaked up to the roof to gather snowballs, then smuggled them downstairs and pelted the doctors. As Thanksgiving approached, Allison was restless to complete her chemo protocol and go home for the holiday. We had promised to release her on Thanksgiving Day in time for her to get home for dinner. She and her father, who was sleeping in her room, sprang out of bed before dawn that morning. Two weeks earlier, Allison had asked Greg to grow a mustache for her. That morning, Allison wanted to shave it off to celebrate their departure from the hospital.

It was just getting light when they finished the shaving, and they decided to watch the dawn from their favorite spot in the hospital. They took the elevator up to a then-deserted terrace on the fourteenth floor that faces east. Huddled together under a blanket, they watched the sun come up red and gold over the river. "It was the best morning of my life," says Greg. "Now every Thanksgiving sunrise is special. When the Lord brings me home to heaven, I think it will be dawn."

When Allison died, a family friend wrote to Jeannie and Greg: "You must feel particularly blessed that Allison lived her whole life as a child." At the time, it seemed to them a strange sentiment to express in a sympathy card, but as the months passed they came to see a lot of truth in it. "I do, in fact, feel particularly blessed," says Jeannie today, five years after Allison's death. "I continue to thank God for the privilege of being Allison's mother. She strengthened me. Her laughter made me want to be funny; her love made me want to be a better mother; her pure faith made mine stronger; and her death made me learn of heaven. She surpassed me and went home first."

TWENTY YEARS AGO, AT THREE IN THE MORNING, I GOT A call from a man I had never met or spoken to before.

"I'm sorry for waking you in the middle of the night," he began, "but it's a matter of life and death."

"That's why I'm in the phone book," I said, turning the receiver away from the bed where Kathy stirred beside me.

"I'm not the kind of person who does this kind of thing, calling strangers in the middle of the night," said the man. "I'm worried that my son is dying."

That conversation was the beginning of my long-lasting friendship with Alan Abramson. As it happened, he was calling from his apartment around the corner from mine in Manhattan. It's not uncommon for neighbors to be strangers in New York City, but there was nothing common about the journey we'd just embarked on.

Earlier that day, Alan's four-year-old son, Jonathan, had been diagnosed with a large brain tumor. Alan spent that day and evening frantically networking and phoning in search of the right doctor. By three in the morning, his search had led him to me. I asked him to bring Jonathan to my office when it opened a few hours later.

Alan describes that day as "stepping into a black, alternate universe." For me, it was another day at work. And yet it stood apart. Jonathan was one of those beautiful kids you can't help but get personally invested in. He was a radiant and energetic redhead with an infectious giggle. Sadly, his kind of tumor—a medulloblastoma—had a grim prognosis at that time. Alan had done his research and quoted the bleak survival statistics to me.

"I've got my own statistics," I told him. "I'm not going to

paint a rosy picture for you. Your family is going into a war—but I'm going to be there with you every step of the way. If we work together, I believe we can beat this."

I refused to believe that Jonathan's tumor couldn't be defeated. Jonathan had his whole life ahead of him, and we took the most aggressive steps to save him. After I removed his tumor, we began radiation treatment to try to contain its malignancy. The next nine months were a horror show for Jonathan, Alan, and his wife, Patti. Alan remembers it as "our reverse gestation, going from life to death. I was supposed to be a source of strength for my son and wife," he says, "but all I wanted to do was crawl into bed and pull the covers over my head."

He didn't crawl into bed. He and his wife put their lives on hold so they could be at Jonathan's side through every minute of his ordeal. Though they had a newborn child, and Alan was in the middle of what had once seemed like vitally important business dealings, they vowed never to leave Jonathan alone in the hospital. NYU had visiting hours in those days, but the Abramsons served notice that they were moving in around the clock. They brought a cot into Jonathan's room, and Alan, Patti, and Elizabeth, a close family friend, tag-teamed through the days and nights. After I had operated on Jonathan's tumor, there wasn't much I could do for the family but sit with them and share their angst. There was nothing comforting to say and no solace to offer, other than my company.

Jonathan suffered terribly. His head was red and peeling from radiation burns. He eventually got to the point where he couldn't eat, so we had to cut a hole in his stomach for a feeding tube. Perhaps because I had become close friends with his parents and was witnessing his pain through their eyes, Jonathan's ordeal made me particularly furious. How could this kind of cruelty be visited on a child? Of course there was no explanation then, and there is no explanation now. There is only the cold fact that some children will become very sick, and some of them will live and some will die—despite all our efforts to save them, and despite all our prayers.

Through it all, Jonathan remained stoic, clear-eyed, and open-hearted. During one of his brief stays at home, some of Jonathan's playmates came over for a visit. Afterward, his father said to him, "Jonathan, you're so lucky to have so many people that really love and care about you." Jonathan thought about it for a moment and then replied matter-of-factly, "I'm not lucky." He wasn't self-pitying, simply self-aware. One day during that period, I had to perform a spinal tap on Jonathan. It's a painful procedure, and most patients, young or old, would have treated me like some kind of sadistic tormentor. What Jonathan did was look up at me from the table and say, "I love you, Dr. Epstein."

Near the end of his life, Jonathan took on a Buddha-like appearance. His head was bald from radiation, his face swollen from steroids. He knew what was happening, and he accepted the approach of his death. I wasn't so brave. I sat with Alan and Patti in his room the night Jonathan died, but I didn't stay to watch him go. I told myself I was giving Alan and Patti some privacy in their grief. The truth is that I couldn't bear to watch that brave little boy die.

Jonathan passed away on the eve of Rosh Hashanah, the Jewish New Year. According to Jewish tradition, children who die on that night bypass the usual passage to heaven. They go straight to the head of the line and sit at the right hand of God. That's what I choose to believe about Jonathan.

No matter how much we loved him, we couldn't save Jonathan. That fact was excruciating to accept. What I didn't realize then was that Jonathan's love, and its healing power, would endure.

I've watched lots of marriages break apart under the pressure of a child's death. As Alan explains, "It put an unimaginable strain on a great marriage. No matter how much you love each other, after you've been through this type of experience it's impossible not to look at your partner and see so much pain that you want to run away." There was a lot of love and strength in their marriage, and they decided to work hard to preserve it. I like to think Jonathan's love had a part in that. Alan and Patti had another child. They moved forward. This year they'll mark their thirtieth wedding anniversary. "We still grieve for Jonathan every day," says Alan. "But we're not bitter anymore. We're incredibly grateful that we had him in our lives for as long as we did."

You'd think that after Jonathan's death, I'd be the last person they'd ever want to see again, and the hospital would be the last place they'd ever want to visit. Instead, they've been close and loyal friends—both to me and to the INN. Our families have become intertwined, like one extended family. When I got the offer to move to Beth Israel, I turned to Alan for counsel and encouragement. He joined the Board of Trustees at the hospital and became the liaison between the board and the INN's medical staff. He worked with Tibet House to bring the Dalai Lama to the INN, and to initiate an exchange of Eastern and Western healing techniques—specifically Eastern meditation and Western diagnostics—that continues today.

Fifteen years after Jonathan's death, Alan and Patti were looking for a way to memorialize his loving spirit. When we began to design the INN, they found it. They discovered the abandoned outdoor terrace on the fourteenth floor of the hospital—the same spot where Allison Trunz and her father had spent their magical Thanksgiving dawn. It wasn't much more than an outdoor storage area that day, but Alan and Patti saw past the piles of broken equipment to the park and esplanade along the East River where Jonathan used to play and laugh. They saw an opportunity to share with other children the view of the park and river Jonathan loved.

So Patti found the designer, and together she and Alan raised the money and oversaw the construction of the Jonathan Parker Abramson Safe Harbor. Their concept was simple: to offer an outdoor sanctuary for families marooned inside an urban hospital, an inviting playground for children who were too sick to visit the park across the street. The Dalai Lama consecrated the terrace as a sanctuary for healing in 1999, and countless children and families have blessed it with their joy since then.

Alan will tell you that Jonathan's love survived his death, that his energy created Safe Harbor and lives on there. "When I visit the terrace," he says, "and I see young patients transformed back into children through play, I think, 'That's because of Jonathan.' When I see their faces tilt up to the sun, see them smile at a boat on the river or point gleefully at a helicopter overhead, I think, 'That's because of Jonathan.' And when I look down at the park by the river where he used to run and play, I like to think he's still hanging out there, trying to bring some of his sunshine into other kids' lives."

THE QUESTION, "WHY DO CHILDREN SUFFER?" HAS NO answer, unless it's simply, "To break our hearts." Once our hearts get broken, they never fully heal. They always ache. But perhaps a broken heart is a more loving instrument. Perhaps only after our hearts have cracked wide open, have finally and totally unclenched, can we truly know love without boundaries.

Epilogue

It's been a year since I revived from my coma. This month, I began going back to work at the INN. I'm here only a couple of afternoons a week now, but I'm hoping to build back up to full time and, if my rehab reaches 100 percent, to get back to the OR. My future role at the INN is still evolving, still a question mark. All I know is that I'm determined to use whatever skills I have to do whatever I can.

My job for the past year has been to rehab my body and mind. In many ways it's been the hardest job of my life. It's given me an even deeper appreciation for the emotional and physical rigors my patients have faced all these years. And it's also given me a poignant insight into the demands it makes on their families.

For most of my adult life I've been in constant motion, shuttling between the OR and patient rounds and tumor boards and medical conferences. This year I've had the rare opportunity to be still, to spend time at home with my family, and to reflect on what I've learned from my practice and from my patients.

I've been on the receiving end of lots of lessons—some tough, some sweet.

After decades of being a patient advocate in negotiations with insurance companies and hospital administrators, I've had a vivid firsthand experience of the extreme fiscal cost of disability. I now know how quickly even the best insurance policies max out, and how expensive treatment suddenly seems when it's coming out of your own pocket.

I've honestly never been excessively attached to my possessions, but I've had to let go of a lot of them recently. A year ago, I owned all the playthings a grown-up boy could desire: a boat, antique cars, and scale-model electric trains, as well as a grand house and art collection. Most of those things are gone, or will be soon—either because they no longer fit in my life or because I can't afford them. I miss some of them a lot—especially my boat—but now that they've left my life, I realize they were never really part of me. They were simply part of what I did for fun when I wasn't working.

Far tougher was losing the professional powers I'd accrued over the course of my career. Literally in the blink of an eye, I lost my life-saving skills as a surgeon, my status as the chief of a world-renowned surgical service, and my earning power as a husband and father. I've missed it all terribly: the great and frightening moments in the OR, the exchange of ideas and research at international conferences, and most of all, the chance to fix what's broken in young patients' lives. I soon learned that no one was going to hand it all back to me, simply because I'd worked so hard to achieve it. I'm going to have to reclaim whatever I can with my one good hand and as much determination as I can muster.

But what's been most instructive to me in this season of loss and recovery has been learning what *can't* be taken away by misfortune.

It's a cliché—and also true—that you really find out who your friends are when you're flat on your back. I've never before been so dependent on the kindness of friends, as well as strangers. Suffice it to say, I've learned who my friends are.

I've spent the last six months almost exclusively at home with my family. My five children, ages fourteen through thirty-two, have taught me hands-on lessons about love this year, each in his or her own way. I have also been blessed with a new granddaughter—and with her birth, I've been reminded that life, like hope, springs eternal.

Throughout my career, I've had a close-up view of marriages bending and often breaking under the strain of a family medical crisis. I have always counted myself lucky to have a strong and loving partner in my wife, Kathy. I now know just how lucky I've been.

My faith in God, and in my own special destiny as a child of God, is undiminished.

So is my determination to continue to heal children in any way I can.

I've drawn a lot of strength recently from being back among our patients at the INN. I've been heartened to discover that some of my former patients have become my colleagues. Danny Trush, the Manhattan Miler who's still refusing to accept labels or limits, is working for Honey Shields as her teen leader in the Child Life department this summer. Bari Stern, another former patient who's now a college sophomore, will be working alongside them. And Lina Orfanos, a patient from twelve years ago and a wonderful musician, is now interning with our music therapist. I'm as proud of these kids as I am of any surgeon I've ever trained. They're my living legacy.

The great gift of this year has been the chance to reconnect through letters, phone calls, and e-mails with patients going back thirty years. Hearing their stories about rebuilding, reclaiming, and renewal in the midst of adversity has been like going back to school for an advanced degree in the art of living. I feel a debt to my young patients that I may never be able to repay. They've repeatedly pointed me down the right path at crucial crossroads, and never more so than in this past year. Since my life capsized, their example and their counsel have been my compass and my lifeboat.

The cards and letters I've received from my patients this year have been a daily tonic for me. One in particular speaks to my current situation. A young woman quoted her Russian grandfather's proverb that guided her when she was a girl recovering from surgery and trying to regain her direction in life: "Only crabs go backwards."

That pretty much nails it for me. I have to go forward, however uncertain the future—which is, after all, what we all have to do. We fool ourselves into thinking we know what the future holds; in reality, none of us knows what pain or pleasure tomorrow will bring. Choosing to go forward in the face of uncertainty is the willful, distinctly human act of optimism we perform each day. We may know too much about the unpredictable ways of the world to expect a happy ending, but we can't help but hope for one all the same.

It's the only way to get to five.

Fred Epstein, M.D.
Institute for Neurology and Neurosurgery
October 21, 2002

Acknowledgments

Naomi's "If I get to five" spirit has sustained us through the challenges of writing this book. There were many dark passages this past year; we'd like to express our appreciation to the individuals who lit the way with their guidance and encouragement.

Our publishing team at Henry Holt stood behind us when we needed them most. They are a caring and focused group of professionals who have earned our gratitude and respect. We thank especially: our publisher, John Sterling, who hung in there with us when the going got tough and who gave us invaluable course corrections when we went astray; our editor, Deborah Brody, who acquired the proposal and lavished her attention and enthusiasm on the manuscript as it evolved; and Jennifer Barth, whose incisive comments made it a better book.

Our loyal and talented agent, Gail Ross, has worn many

hats throughout the creation of this book—all of them with great style. Tim Sullivan at Dan Klores Communications has been a steadfast ally throughout, for which we thank him.

Kathy Epstein stepped up and played a pivotal editorial role that she never signed up for, in a year when many unexpected duties fell on her shoulders. We want to credit her and thank her for the long hours and many insights she contributed. Heartfelt thanks go to Alan and Patti Abramson for their unstinting friendship—always treasured, but never more so than in this difficult year.

Several people read the manuscript at critical stages and contributed valuable comments, including Dana Davis, Hedi Levine, and Tony Horwitz. Special thanks to Elinor Horwitz for her excellent line edits, to Stephen Mills for his acuity of mind and spirit, and to Kemp Battle for his expert winnowing of the trees in the forest.

The extended family of the INN has been the unseen support team for this book. Our particular thanks to Eileen O'Donnell, Tania Shiminski-Maher, and Honey Shields. And thanks to the Making Headway Foundation for the care and comfort it provides to the children at the INN.

Finally, and most importantly, we want to thank the young people and their families who bravely and candidly shared their personal stories. The contributions of many patients couldn't be included in this short book, but all of them have been our valued and deeply appreciated collaborators. Their courage and character have inspired the writing of this book at every stage.

About the Authors

FRED EPSTEIN, M.D., is the founding director of the Institute for Neurology and Neurosurgery (INN) at Beth Israel Hospital in New York City. His groundbreaking surgical techniques and his commitment to humane patient care have saved thousands of children's lives and earned him a reputation as one of the world's leading pediatric neurosurgeons. Dr. Epstein lives with his wife and two of his five children in Greenwich, Connecticut.

JOSHUA HORWITZ is the president of Living Planet Books, a book-packaging firm in Washington, D.C., where he lives with his wife and three daughters. He is the coauthor of *Wrestling with Angels,* and the author of several children's books.